W9-DGV-364

Rosie's Mom

FORGOTTEN WOMEN WORKERS OF THE FIRST WORLD WAR

For
EVERY
FIGHTER
a
WOMAN
WORKER
UNITED
WAR
WORK
CAMPAIGN
CARE
for
HER
through The YWCA
ADOLPH
TREIDLER

Rosie's Mom

FORGOTTEN WOMEN WORKERS OF THE FIRST WORLD WAR

Carrie Brown

NORTHEASTERN UNIVERSITY PRESS
Boston

Northeastern University Press

Library of Congress Cataloging-in-Publication Data

Brown, Carrie.
Rosie's mom : forgotten women workers of the First World War / Carrie Brown.
p. cm.
Includes bibliographical references and index.
ISBN 1-55553-535-6 (cloth : alk. paper)
1. Women—Employment—United States—History—20th century. 2. World War, 1914–1918—Women—United States. I. Title.
HD6095 .B737 2002
331.4′0973′09041—dc21 2002007483

Designed by Joyce C. Weston

Composed in Perpetua by Joyce C. Weston.
Printed and bound by Thomson-Shore, Inc., Dexter, Michigan.
The paper is Fortune Matte, an acid-free stock.

MANUFACTURED IN THE UNITED STATES OF AMERICA
06 05 04 03 02 5 4 3 2 1

Frontispiece: A poster by Adolph Treidler urging financial support for women war workers. Courtesy of Archives and Special Collections, University of Nebraska–Lincoln Libraries.

TO GALEN AND GAVIN

WITH LOVE FROM

THEIR MOM

Contents

Rosie's Mom

In 1917, a full generation before Rosie the Riveter rolled up her sleeves and adorned the cover of the *Saturday Evening Post,* American women entered the workshops of the First World War. Trading their ankle-length skirts for coarse bloomers or overalls, they built fabric-covered biplanes, hauled scrap metal, filled hand grenades with powder, made gas masks, processed meat to send to the troops, and helped keep the freight trains running. By filling men's places, at less than men's wages, they helped win the war. And then they were forgotten. During the Second World War, "Rosie the Riveter" posters, magazine articles, songs, movies, and stage shows would celebrate the accomplishments and encourage the efforts of women ordnance workers. Those images—images of women doing difficult and remarkable things during World War II—remain in our collective memory. But Rosie was not the first, and the World War II images are not the first to record women's industrial war work. This is the story of Rosie's Mom.

Rosie's Mom

FORGOTTEN WOMEN WORKERS OF THE FIRST WORLD WAR

CHAPTER ONE

Prelude: Forgotten Women

On a winter's morning in 1916, Nellie stood for the first time before a cartridge heading machine. A floppy cap covered and confined her upswept hair. A pair of coarse, bloomer-style overalls—womanalls they called them—gave an unaccustomed freedom to her legs. Nineteen years old, fresh from the rugged life on a New Hampshire farm, Nellie knew hard work, and she knew long hours. But she had never before confronted a machine larger than herself, a machine that shook her whole body with its vibrations. She had never before handled caustic chemicals or fed percussion caps—already loaded with explosive powder—into a quick-running machine. And she had never before seen an unexpected explosion hurl a woman across the room. During the next two years, she would see or do all of these.[1]

At the Union Metallic Cartridge factory, the farm girl became a munitions worker, her feet firmly planted on the shop floor, her hands and eyes intent on turning out as many cartridges as possible in a ten-hour shift. She had taken on this new job not for her country, since the United States had not yet entered the war, but for herself and her family. At first it was simply a question of a few more dollars in the weekly pay envelope. By the end of 1918, munitions work for Nellie—and for a million women like her—would become a patriotic duty. The feverish pace of production and the frequent industrial accidents would be among the sacrifices made by people on the home front, while American soldiers fought and died on the other side of the Atlantic.

Nellie was surrounded by women who had previously worked in other trades. Helen had pasted together paper boxes. Susan Jones had operated a power sewing machine to make men's clothing. Others had dipped chocolate candies by hand, or clerked in department stores, or cleaned the homes of the wealthy as live-in maids. And so the story of women war workers begins not in a munitions factory, but on the farms and at the candy companies, in the sweatshops and the garment factories where they worked before the war. It begins with young girls working in textile mills and canneries, before the social costs of child labor were calculated by the more comfortable middle class. It begins also in the homes where married women took in washing, and where they cooked for boarders as part of the struggle to feed their own children. And it begins on the street corners where workers listened to the messengers of trade unionism, socialism, and even revolution.

Women had, of course, been working in American factories since the early nineteenth century, when the invention of large textile machines took spinning and weaving out of the home and into the factory. Before that, for thousands of years, women had cared for livestock, raised gardens, made the family's bread, knitted their socks, and sewed their clothes. The entire family had worked together as an economic unit. Then came the spinning jennies and the looms, and the beginning of a separation between home life and work, both for men and for women. By 1860, factories produced not just thread and yarn and woven fabrics, but also cheap ready-to-wear clothing, gloves, and caps, all made on newly invented sewing and knitting machines. Soon large food-processing plants took over the canning of foods, and the meat packing houses of Chicago processed and preserved beef and pork. By the beginning of the twentieth century, the job of feeding and clothing the nation had been industrialized. For the prosperous middle-class family, the remaining heavy housework could be handled by hired help. The middle-class American wife, then, had leisure for music, reading, religious study, and charity work. The wives of white, American-born,

This little spinner, who was only four feet three inches tall, admitted that she was working illegally at a cotton mill in North Carolina. Photograph by Lewis Hine, courtesy of the National Archives at College Park (102-LH-462).

skilled workers bore a heavier burden of housework, but still generally hoped to avoid working for wages. The stay-at-home wife was the ideal, and American working families achieved it with some success in prosperous times, and with less success during periods of family crisis or economic depression.

Who, then, made the clothing and processed the food and assembled all the new consumer goods for the middle and upper classes? A crush of immigrants, mostly passing through Ellis Island, filled the factories and sweatshops of America. Between 1865 and 1916, 27 million people entered the United States from abroad.[2] Some few from the British Isles spoke English, but the vast numbers from southern and eastern Europe brought with them a profusion of other

Sorting rags for a paper company. Photograph by Lewis Hine, courtesy of George Eastman House (GEH 7840).

languages. Their lack of English and their often inappropriate work skills put new immigrants at the bottom of the economic ladder. Former agricultural workers canned foods in the city; Italian women accustomed to doing fine embroidery found themselves doing coarse needlework in sweatshops, or sorting rags in dark basement workrooms; schoolteachers who spoke Russian and Yiddish ended up toiling in the overpopulated garment district of the Lower East Side of New York.

In San Francisco, the port of entry for Chinese immigrants, women who managed to avoid forced prostitution could find work picking shrimp for six cents a pound or doing hand sewing.[3] A rare few found lighter work in the service industries in Chinatown. In the Southwest, Mexican women worked in the fields, as did black women in the old South. The industrial work of the nation, however, was still largely done in the cities of Northeast and the upper Midwest by immigrants of European descent.

The flood of labor into those cities kept wages low and rents high. Immigrant districts were closely packed with seven-, eight-, and nine-story tenement buildings. High above the street, laundry fluttered on clotheslines that crisscrossed between the buildings. In summer, children slept on the fire escapes or on top of the chicken coops in the alleyways, and pillows and featherbeds bulged from the windows and hung on the railings. In winter, everyone crowded indoors, where an extended family shared a two- or three-room apartment, with perhaps a child or a boarder even sleeping in the kitchen. There might be one shared bath on a hall, or there might be only a cold-water sink, with the toilet out in the yard.

Mrs. Battaglia, whose husband was crippled by a fall, worked in a shop Monday through Friday. On Saturday she worked at home, sewing men's pants, with the help of Tessie (age twelve) and Tony (age seven). Photograph by Lewis Hine, courtesy of the National Archives at College Park (102-LH-1A).

If a married man happened to be unskilled, disabled, intemperate, or just unlucky, his wages most often would not support his family. Then the women and children picked up the burden. The kitchen served as a workroom where mothers and their preschool-aged children made artificial flowers, picked nut meats from the shells, or pulled basting stitches from piles of overcoats that had been trundled home in carts or baby buggies. Older children, after school, could help bring in a few pennies doing the family work around the kitchen table. Sometimes the children left school early and went to work illegally. At the Triangle Shirtwaist factory in New York, when the state factory inspector came around, the children were hidden in boxes under piles of clothing as the inspector passed through,[4] while in southern textile mills, underage children were openly employed. In major industrial centers around the country, three-fourths of the children left school without completing the seventh grade.[5]

When they left school, the boys sought out apprenticeships, or at least entered factories where they would work alongside older, skilled men and could learn a trade. The girls went into "women's trades," where training consisted of a few hours, or a few minutes, of instruction in how to do one particular task—by hand or on a machine—and to do it as rapidly as possible, for ten or twelve or fourteen hours a day. The process of making one item was subdivided into many small tasks, and as long as each girl had to do only one of those tasks, ignorance of English was not a problem. Supervisors had little to explain: work quickly, don't stop.

Many native-born daughters of working-class families joined the immigrant girls in the factories, leaving school in their midteens because no one expected them to stay, helping out their families with a few extra dollars a week, waiting to see what else life had to offer. At the turn of the century, of the 5 million women who worked for wages, half were under the age of twenty-five.[6] For the most part, the factories were filled with row upon row of girls in various stages of having the giddiness of adolescence drained out of them by long, tedious work.

If the girls looked around them, they could see a few married women, and some who were divorced or widowed, but still the American-born and the immigrant girls both expected marriage and children to release them from the factory. A Yiddish song expressed their dream:

Day the same as night, night the same as day,
And all I do is sew and sew and sew.

Seated on a rough wooden box, eight-year-old Daisy Langford placed caps on cans at the rate of forty per minute. Photograph by Lewis Hine taken in Seaford, Delaware, in 1910. Courtesy of the National Archives at College Park (102-LH-1593).

> *May God help me and my love come soon,*
> *That I may leave this work and go.*[7]

And generally marriage *would* release them, except that all too often married life would be punctuated by periods of home work or factory work.

The work itself was almost entirely mechanical. In a cannery in Pittsburgh, cans of beans traveled on a conveyor belt past a row of young girls. As the cans passed, inexorably moving at the pace of the conveyor, the girls would slip a piece of pork into each can. One can, one piece of pork, for ten hours a day, six days a week.[8] The worker became another arm of the machine, with no control over speed, no opportunity for a rest. A button-covering machine completed a button in a few seconds, and the new pieces had to be added in rhythm to keep up

When there was work to be done, shrimp pickers in Mississippi toiled from three in the morning to three or four in the afternoon. Photograph by Lewis Hine, courtesy of the National Archives at College Park (102-LH-2033).

with the machine. A paper box–molding machine opened and closed thirty times in a minute. A flat ironing machine pressed sheets and tablecloths at forty or fifty feet a minute while women fed the linens in by hand.[9] Where the pace was not driven by machine, workers were paid by the piece, and they needed to keep a quick and steady rate simply to make enough for food and rent. At a wholesale millinery factory, a quick woman could make a dozen hats in a day; and in a cigarette factory, an experienced packer could pack 35,000 to 40,000 cigarettes in a nine- or ten-hour day.[10] In one fruit-canning factory, as the employer led a visitor through the plant, he paused near a group of four Hungarian women who pared quinces. "They are the best workers I have," he boasted. "They keep at it just like horses." [11]

Most of the women's trades were seasonal. Food had to be canned just after harvest; candies needed to be fresh for the Christmas and Easter trades; winter cloaks were lined with fur only when they could be sold and not stored; hats could be designed only after the latest style was announced in Paris. In the busy season, "girls wanted" signs—in Hebrew, English, and Italian—cluttered the entrances to factories. Workrooms hummed with machinery. Girls crowded around long tables, putting in twelve- to sixteen-hour days—often at no extra pay for overtime. The employers and foremen hurried about, urging workers to a faster pace. Then, a few weeks later, the shops would be nearly empty, the machines would be silent, and the women would be searching for new work, often not finding it.[12] In the year 1900, nearly one-quarter of the American work force was unemployed for some part of the year.[13] Mimi, an Italian girl in New York, worked at sewing underwear for eight months, spent four months idle, then made lampshades for

A day's washing was a major task that involved heating water in a washtub over a gas stove. From the Women's Bureau, courtesy of the National Archives at College Park (RG 86G-6U-2).

a year, then had another idle period of several months, then addressed envelopes for two months before being laid off again.[14] Lisa Hasanovitz held forty jobs in four years, spending one desperate period in a sweater knitting shop where "the dust and lint from the wool were inhaled instead of air. I could hardly speak in the evening," she said, "my throat would be so clogged with wool."[15] Others simply waited for their accustomed trade to begin hiring again, and spent the long weeks of unemployment hungry and worried.

Even when women did have work, the wages often kept them at the edge of starvation. Earning four or five dollars a week, a girl could just afford food, clothing, and carfare. There was nothing left for medical care, savings, or recreation. If she worked in the garment trades, she also had to buy her own needles and to pay for the power used by her sewing machine. In some factories, she was expected to provide her own sewing machine, which could cost two months' pay. Each day, she carried the machine on her back to and from work. If she complained about her wage or her treatment, the foreman would simply send her on her way. Another worker could be hired and trained within hours. If she arrived for work late, she might find herself locked out or forced to give up half a day's pay. Men—even unskilled men—earned nearly twice as much; and the skilled craftsmen had unions that protected both their wages and their hours. The young women—unskilled, uneducated, planning to work only a few years—and the older women—still unskilled and surrounded by teenagers—had no unions, no protectors, and no economic power.

In the chaos of this new industrial world, working women coped as best they could. They developed support systems in their families and ethnic communities. They switched jobs whenever a few pennies more could be made at a new factory. They took in washing or brought hand sewing home at night. But they were exhausted. When they had children, the children were undernourished and undereducated. Their workplaces were often filthy and dangerous. Foremen, who knew how little they earned, offered them a week's wages for an hour's indiscretion, and men in shops and on the streets accosted them and offered money for sexual favors. The established trade unions ignored them, and the politicians claimed that most women worked for "pin money." Finally, just as America headed into the twentieth century, women began to find new ways to help each other.

The daughters of the middle and upper classes may have been coddled and privileged, but they were not asleep. Graduating from prestigious women's colleges, they had been educated for a world that was not quite ready to receive them. A few elbowed their way into the professions of their fathers and brothers—business, medicine, and law. Others sought something new, where being female would be less of an obstacle, and where they could have some impact upon the world. As they looked around them, these socially conscious women saw mothers who worked in the factory for twelve hours and then came home to a full evening of housework. They found men who had been injured or

At this cotton mill in Vermont, the children pictured ranged in age from twelve to fifteen. When the war came a few years later, 30 percent of young men would be declared medically unfit for military service. In 1910, social reformers had already begun to claim that overwork, malnutrition, and industrial disease would make working women unfit for childbearing. Photograph by Lewis Hine, courtesy of the National Archives at College Park (102-LH-1052).

Photograph by Lewis Hine, 1912. His caption reads, in part, "8pm and not yet finished. The little one on left is not yet 4 years old, yet she works on flowers all day and sometimes until 8 or 9 pm." Courtesy of the National Archives at College Park (102-LH-2875).

maimed in industrial accidents and had no insurance or worker's compensation to get their families through the rough times. They saw children leaving school at age thirteen or fourteen to help put food on the table. They heard about shop girls drifting into prostitution because they could not survive on their meager wages.[16] Here was a field for action. Imbued with the late-Victorian cultural ideal of woman as guardian of the family and morality, and stirred by their own lack of full citizenship, women who did not need to work developed strong feelings of sisterhood with women who did.

Although they had no real political power, middle- and upper-class white women nevertheless wielded a good bit of influence. When the General Federation of Women's Clubs made up its mind that Congress should investigate the working conditions of women and children, the wives of senators pressured their husbands to appropriate the money. Said one senator, "My wife . . . telegraphed me to get busy, and all her friends did the same."[17] Through another organization, the National Consumers' League (NCL), women found that their purchasing power gave them some small influence over shop and factory conditions. The NCL first established "white lists" and league labels of approval to help housewives select goods produced under humane conditions. After a few years, the NCL began to lobby for laws that would more directly protect women workers.

These reform-minded women were not simply soft-hearted agitators sending telegrams and boycotting department stores. Jane Addams and other intellectuals moved into settlement houses in poor neighborhoods, determined to help the lower classes by living among them. Addams worried especially about the adolescent girls sent out to find work and entertainment in cities that were growing rapidly and in industries that were controlled by neither government regulation nor social conscience. "Never before in civilization," she warned in her book *The Spirit of Youth and the City Streets,* "have such numbers of young girls been suddenly released from the protection of the home and permitted to walk unattended upon city streets and to work under alien roofs."[18] At Hull House in Chicago and other settlement houses around the country, middle-class reformers provided English classes for immigrants, medical care for the poor, teas and dances for restless adolescents, day-care centers for the children of working mothers, and meeting places for fledgling unions. In San Francisco, the Chinese Women's Jeleab Association taught literacy, sewing, and self-reliance.[19] African American women established social clubs and homes for young women who had migrated to the cities to find work. A few settlement houses and women's clubs in three or four cities could not, however, meet the needs of the growing population of desperate and destitute families. The American people in general needed to be mobilized.

Well-educated women of a scientific bent put their training in economics and sociology to work on behalf of the poor. They inspected the factories, and then visited the workers in their homes, traveling along the dirty streets, through the mud and up the rickety staircases into cramped and uncleanable apartments. Then they published their reports, filled with hard data on wages, rents, family structures, apartment sizes, and the number of children who worked. At the

When Mary Van Kleeck investigated the millinery trade, she found that workers typically put in fifty to fifty-five hours a week. Photograph by Lewis Hine, courtesy of George Eastman House (GEH 5129).

Russell Sage Foundation, a new organization devoted to social research, this work was organized by Mary Van Kleeck.

The Van Kleecks had been in New York since the days when it was New Amsterdam, and claimed at least one ancestor who served in the Continental Army under General Washington. Mary Van Kleeck's father and grandfather were Episcopal ministers, and her education at Smith College had only reinforced her sense of social duty. Rational, efficient, and well organized, she became the prototypical industrial investigator: a scholar with a conscience. In 1908, at the age of twenty-five, she had stated her manifesto: "On the wall of a factory building in Bond Street, there is a sign which reads, 'This floor will sustain an evenly distributed load of 125 lbs. to each square foot.' No such definite statement exists regarding the sustaining power of the men and women employed in the factory." Her field of social research would attempt to discover and articulate those limits.[20]

In the factories and tenements of New York, Mary Van Kleeck found women and girls on the point of breaking. Along with her colleagues at the Russell Sage Foundation, she produced reports on millinery workers, artificial flower makers, bookbinders, Italian women in New York, and the working women of Pittsburgh.

Their data put meat on the bones of the argument for laws that would protect the weakest workers. Allying themselves with a few sympathetic state legislators, lawyers, and congressmen, women worked to pass maximum hour and minimum wage laws, and restrictions on child labor and night work. And when an Oregon law restricting women to a ten-hour day was challenged as unconstitutional, Josephine Goldmark of the National Consumers' League, armed with data collected by the social investigators, helped attorney Louis Brandeis write a brief to present to the Supreme Court. The court finally decided in favor of the ten-hour law, claiming that the larger interest of society outweighed the individual's right to negotiate freely in the marketplace: "As healthy mothers are essential to vigorous offspring," the opinion read, "the physical well-being of women becomes an object of public interest and care in order to preserve the strength and vigor of the race."[21]

The most powerful expression of sisterly solidarity took the form of an organization designed to help working women help themselves: the Women's Trade Union League. It was an odd organization. Founded by members of the upper class and run by daughters of the privileged and powerful, it nonetheless encouraged the development of trade unions, and it affiliated itself with the

American Federation of Labor. Along with Sunday afternoon teas and discussions, along with organizing clubs and setting up lunchrooms in factories, the Women's Trade Union League encouraged working women to join existing unions or form new ones. It taught them how to run a meeting using parliamentary procedure. It gave them opportunities for public speaking. It printed leaflets explaining the benefits of collective bargaining or outlining existing labor laws. It helped infant unions establish dues and election policies. And when workers went on strike, the WTUL provided food for their families, halls for their meetings, and lawyers and bail for arrested picketers.

Margaret Dreier Robins, for years the president of the National WTUL, clearly stated the reformers' most basic goal: the salvation of America through social reform.

> The nature of the attack of modern industrial despotism upon the integrity and promise of our individual and national life is such as makes a special call upon the women of our country, and it seems to have been reserved for this generation to work out a new basis for our industrial civilization. Freedom, maternity, education, and morality—all the blessed and abiding interests of childhood and the home—are at issue in this supreme struggle. All women who honor their sex and love their country should unite with us and our working sisters in the struggle for industrial freedom.[22]

The WTUL quickly attracted working women who, though lacking education, had brains, political savvy, and organizational skills. Rose Schneiderman and Mary Anderson—a cap maker and a shoe worker—would be among the women launched by the WTUL into national affairs.

As they built alliances through women's clubs, the Consumers' League, and the WTUL, women began to have hope. Peaceful reform *could* remove the threat of class warfare. Women's health *could* be protected. Women's voices *could* be heard. Suffrage *could* be won. Nineteenth-century feminists had argued for the ballot in terms of their rights as citizens in a democracy. In the early twentieth century, they would argue that woman suffrage was needed to protect "the mothers of the race." Working across class lines, women hoped to improve their own lot and at the same time to humanize industrial America.

Then came the First World War. Suddenly, the nation needed more food, more weapons, and more military clothing and supplies. It needed nurses and

A telephone exchange in Lynchburg, Virginia, around 1900. Courtesy of the National Archives at College Park (RG 86G-10F-14).

typists and telephone operators. Leaders of women's organizations realized that the war brought both a threat and a promise. Would the crisis erode working conditions, pushing women even further toward ill health and exhaustion? Or would it bring the chance for new jobs and new training? Would war bring women a stronger role in American political life? If women gave their very best efforts to the cause, would anyone remember, afterward, what they did to help win the war?

While they waited to discover the answers to these questions, each woman had to find her own way to serve in a country at war. White middle- and upper-class women had the most dramatic options. Some went to France as telephone and telegraph operators, as Red Cross nurses and ambulance drivers. At the overseas military camps, Salvation Army "lassies" set up canteens and made doughnuts for homesick American soldiers. Most of the women who went to Europe were young, single, and financially well-off: able to work without pay, willing to buy their own uniforms and equipment, available to leave their homes for service overseas.[23] On the home front, too, millions of upper- and middle-class women mobilized. College students went out to the farms to harvest the crops; housewives knitted socks for soldiers, planted gardens, and organized food conservation drives. Society women gave up their teas and their routine charity work to drive cars and ambulances for the Army's training bases. Well-to-do black women organized to provide supplies and recreation for the neglected soldiers of their own race.

Women who worked for wages were a group apart: they were already putting in ten- and twelve-hour days, just to survive. Volunteering was not an option. But when the war brought new demands for American industry, and high wages for those willing to take on war work, these women were ready. Moving quickly into the arsenals and munitions factories, they joined the men who stayed behind to produce the machinery of war.

The pages that follow will trace their journey, from the women's trades to the war industries and back again. Each chapter highlights a particular city or particular kind of work, chosen because it best illustrates the changes in working women's lives during a given year. Together the scraps of individual biography, the city histories, and the vignettes from selected workshops create a larger story, the story of a group of ordinary and mostly anonymous women who, through their adaptability and courage, would help their country win the war.

Born into working-class families in the last years of the nineteenth century or the first years of the twentieth, these women learned at an early age that they needed to work if they wanted to eat. They also learned that keeping a job would not always be easy and that striving for higher wages would not always be safe, for they found themselves in an uncertain and dangerous world. In those years, the struggle between labor and capital was at its most violent and contentious. Indeed, when the trouble began in Europe, America already had trouble enough at home.

CHAPTER TWO

Bread or Revolution: New York, 1913–1914

FROM THE BEGINNING OF THE century, national rivalries had kept Europe in turmoil. France was bitter about territorial losses to Germany; Russia and Serbia encouraged Slavs to withdraw from the Austro-Hungarian Empire; and all of the large nations feuded over influence in China and Africa. In 1912, open war in the Balkans gave Austria more reason to worry about the permanence of its borders, and so in 1913 the great powers of Europe tried to impose a solution on the Balkans. Meeting in London, they created an independent Albania, cutting Serbia off from the sea.

■

Rose Schneiderman stood only four and a half feet tall, so a mere soap box wouldn't do. For street meetings, she stood on a ladder, which was carried from one factory entrance to another. With her unruly red hair pulled back in a bun, and her crisp white shirtwaist tucked neatly into a long, dark skirt, the tiny woman climbed up onto her ladder and unfurled her trade union banner. Her round face flushed with passion, she spoke in Yiddish and in English, calling on the young women in the garment trades to join together and demand better treatment and a living wage. When she spoke about woman's need for voting rights, she made grown men laugh, and as she continued, her pathos and passion could make them cry.[1] In 1910 and 1913 she helped organize major strikes of garment workers in New York City. And in 1914, without her ladder, she traveled to Washington for a meeting with the president of the United States. She looked up at the tall, gray-templed Woodrow Wilson and told him that while he worried about the war in Europe, there was an industrial war going on in his own country. She knew that war well, because she had been living in the middle of it, trying to find a way to peace.[2]

She had been born in a small village in Russian-occupied Poland in 1882, at a time when the Russian empire was changing rapidly. Industrialization was transforming the cities, and revolution simmered just below the autocratic surface. In an effort to retain the loyalty of the majority, the government stirred up hatred against the Jews. Anti-Semitic edicts and violent pogroms drove Jews from one town to another, and eventually drove many of them out of Europe altogether. Between 1881 and 1924, two million Eastern European Jews would migrate to the United States,[3] and the Schneiderman family was in one of the first waves. In 1890, Samuel Schneiderman stole away and traveled alone to the magical land of America. Then, a few months later, he sent money to bring the rest of the family across the sea. Because they had no passports, the mother and children had to sneak across the border into Germany. Guided by a paid agent, they crossed at night on foot, carrying on their backs a few odds and ends of clothing, cooking utensils, bed linens, and the family's precious samovar—so that they could make Russian tea in the New World. On the passage across the Atlantic—crowded into steerage with hundreds of others—everyone in the family was seasick, and one of the children came down with measles. Finally they arrived—and soon settled—in New York. There the eldest child, a daughter, changed her name from Rachel to the more American Rose. She learned English quickly in the American schools, but her father died in 1892, just two years after the family arrived in America. And so young Rose went to work early, first at home sewing, next in a department store running cash between the sales clerk and the cashier, and then in a factory, making men's caps on a sewing machine.

At Fox and Lederer's cap factory, Rose Schneiderman and her companions began to realize that the men in the trade, because of their union, got better treatment and better wages than women. The women knew that they would never be allowed into the men's branches of the union, and so they determined

Rose Schneiderman in 1908. Courtesy of Rose Schneiderman Photograph Collection, Tamiment Institute Library, New York University.

to form a women's group: "Bravely we ventured into the office of the United Cloth Hat and Cap Makers Union and told the man in charge that we would like to be organized. . . . We were told that we would have to have at least twenty-five women from a number of factories before we could acquire a charter."[4] Twenty-five signatures came very quickly to the persuasive Rose Schneiderman. They soon had their charter, and suddenly her evenings were filled with shop meetings, and her Sunday afternoons with lectures. She emerged from the loneliness of overworked adolescence into a world of fellowship with other workers, all striving for the right to organize and to better themselves. During the lunch hour, they would gather around her machine and talk about the union and a bright future when they would "live under a socialist form of government and poverty would be a thing of the past."[5] In 1904—at the age of only twenty-two—Rose Schneiderman was elected the first woman member of the executive board of the cap makers' union.

Then in 1905 her life changed again, when she discovered the Women's Trade Union League. Founded only a year before by middle- and upper-class reformers, the WTUL had quickly developed a strong New York branch determined to draw women into trade unions, to train them for leadership, and to support them during strikes. In 1908, Rose Schneiderman became the WTUL's first paid Jewish organizer, working with women in the garment trades on the Lower East Side. It was not easy work. Organizing girls in the ever-shifting needle trades was like "trying to organize the wind."[6] Then there were the bosses. When a group of paper-box makers had formed a union in 1904, the employers forced all workers to sign an oath, promising not to join. In turn, the bosses promised that any woman who set foot in the union hall would be fired.[7]

The bosses were not the only ones who frowned upon young women joining unions. Rose Schneiderman's mother complained that a union organizer would never find a husband. Rose would be far too busy with all of her meetings. Besides, what man would want a woman who stood on a ladder on the street corner and harangued passers-by? Other parents felt the same. Respectable women simply did not behave this way.[8]

Schneiderman was too busy to care. She had her first successes in the white-goods trade. White goods—corsets and other unmentionable undergarments—required little skill. Often an immigrant girl found her first job in a white-goods factory, and so the shops were filled with young teenagers still wearing short skirts, with their hair hanging down their backs in long braids. Sadie Aronovitch, a typical worker, tacked pink ribbons onto corset covers—thirty-nine corsets a day, twelve hours a day, six days a week. At twenty dollars a month, she actually earned a little more than some of the other girls. A young immigrant alone in the city, she paid three dollars a month for a shared bed in a rented room. Twenty-five cents a day bought her a roll and a cup of coffee for breakfast, a sandwich for lunch, and dinner in a cheap basement café. After buying clothes and incidentals, and paying for the thread and power used by her sewing machine at the factory, she had a few dollars left to send to her family back in Russia.[9]

The short skirt on the paper-box maker in the foreground identifies her as a very young teen, perhaps working illegally. Photograph by Lewis Hine, courtesy of the National Archives at College Park (102-LH-584).

Small subcontractors, taking in piecework from larger garment companies, operated in dingy rooms in the tenements. Women's Bureau photograph, courtesy of the National Archives at College Park (RG 86G-2A-3).

When a group of young women at Milgrim Brothers—a maker of women's muslin underwear—spontaneously walked out to protest a cut in their piece rate, they went to the WTUL for help. Rose Schneiderman immediately organized picket lines and began talking to them about how to make a union work. Within a couple of weeks, she had managed to persuade the owners to restore the former piece rate. More important, Milgrim agreed that in future conflicts, they would deal with a grievance committee selected by the workers. Now both the owners and the workers would have an alternative to the strike as a way of settling their differences.[10]

Next came the Aptheker shop, where the workers won the same concessions. In this case, the issue of sexual harassment—a widespread problem in women's industries—also had to be addressed. Mr. Aptheker had a habit of pinching the girls as he passed by them during the day. Rose Schneiderman told him "that this business of pinching the girls in the rear was not nice, that the girls resented it, and would he please stop it." He looked at her in amazement and claimed "Why, Miss Schneiderman, these girls are like my children." The shop chairwoman spoke up quickly and coldly: "Mr. Aptheker we'd rather be orphans."[11] The pinching stopped. These small shop-by-shop successes, however, did little for the trade as a whole. The white-goods workers were of many nationalities and backgrounds—Russians, Romanians, Italians, Syrians, Turks, and Greeks.[12] They could barely communicate with each other, they knew nothing about unions, and they were very young.

Before she could begin on a citywide campaign for the white-goods workers, Rose Schneiderman was called away. In the winter of 1909–1910, New York's shirtwaist makers went on strike, and the WTUL would have to help

A striking garment worker being arrested in Chicago, 1910. Photograph courtesy of the Chicago Historical Society (ICHi-04937).

them. The waistmakers, too, were almost all young and unmarried. Two-thirds of them were Jewish immigrants from Eastern Europe and Russia; the rest were mostly Italians, and there were a few—but very few—blacks. All of these women suffered under an accumulation of insults, fines, and petty tyranny, along with filth and overcrowding in the shops. Worst of all, an economic depression had driven wages down. With little support from the International Ladies Garment Workers Union (ILGWU), which had only four dollars in its local treasury, the waistmakers "stood up and brushed the threads off their dresses and walked away" from the only thing that stood between them and starvation. "Starve quick, or we'll starve slow" was their motto.[13] Twenty thousand waistmakers—some reports said thirty or even forty thousand—walked out that winter.

In their thin coats and flimsy shoes, they picketed in the snow. They were beaten and arrested, fined and jailed. But they were also supported by the Women's Trade Union League. Rose Schneiderman rushed in to help organize meetings and picket duty and to call up the volunteers. It was in this strike that the "mink brigade" first appeared on the picket line. Society matrons, students from Vassar, and the daughters of prominent politicians, judges, and financiers showed up to lend their support. When Anne Morgan, the daughter of J. P. Morgan, visited the strikers, she caught the attention of a reporter from the *New York Times,* and her opinion appeared in the paper the next day: "These conditions are terrible, and the girls must be helped to organize and keep up their organizations."[14] Alva Belmont, from one of the four hundred wealthiest families in the city, spent an evening at the courthouse watching young strikers face fines and imprisonment. Her conclusions were also reported in the *New York Times.* "There are women," she claimed, "who have no rights which man or law or society recognize."[15] Even more support came to the strike when three young Vassar women took on the job of publicity committee and kept the strike on the front page of the newspapers for weeks.[16]

When the mink brigade mingled with the working girls, the police and the companies' hired guards held back in the use of their clubs. Fewer ribs were broken, and fewer girls showed up at the police station with blood on their faces. The well-to-do allies also hired lawyers, paid the bail for arrested strikers, and served as witnesses in court.

Meanwhile, Rose Schneiderman went to Boston, taking with her a sixteen-year-old waistmaker, Rose Perr, who had spent thirty days in the penitentiary simply for picketing. They spoke in Faneuil Hall, where they stunned the audi-

A modern, but crowded, garment factory. Photograph by Lewis Hine, courtesy of George Eastman House (GEH 5141).

ence with their tale of meager wages and twelve-hour days, of arbitrary arrests and police brutality. Schneiderman then continued the tour alone, speaking at Radcliffe, Wellesley, and Mount Holyoke, and at union meetings in industrial centers around Massachusetts. She traveled alone by train, slept in a different hotel room every night for four weeks, and walked boldly through barrooms to get to union meetings. All together she raised ten thousand dollars in donations for the strike fund.[17]

When the shirtwaist strike spread to Philadelphia, manufacturers began to look for a settlement.[18] After eleven weeks of hunger and uncertainty, the shirtwaist makers went back to work with shorter hours and a reduction in fees and fines. The employers had refused, however, to recognize the unions or to set up any procedures for settling grievances or improving overall conditions. It was progress, but small progress. And in some of the shops, no settlement was reached at all.

Still, the country was stunned by the ability of young, inexperienced women to sustain such a fight. Over the next few months, the country would be stunned again—this time by the futility of it all. A strike might win shorter hours or higher pay, but it alone could not transform a chaotic industry made up of thousands of little shops, each trying to undercut the others. And it could do little for the overcrowding and unsafe conditions in the factory. The danger of those conditions finally, in the year following the strike, became impossible to ignore.

First, disaster occurred in Newark, in a building that had been standing since before the Civil War. It had been a gun shop, then a machine shop, and its floors were soaked with oil. According to the Newark Fire Exchange, it was "an especially hazardous fire risk," and yet it possessed only two fire escapes, when it should have had a dozen. In November of 1910, the building housed two paper-box factories, a muslin underwear shop, and a lamp shop. Nearly four hundred women were at work on a Saturday morning when, somehow, some spilled gasoline in the lamp shop ignited. Within minutes, fire spread through the third floor and into the stairwell leading to the fourth floor. As the women rushed to the windows, a small interior set of steps—designed to help them reach the window fire escape—collapsed, cutting off one of the iron escape ladders. At the second fire escape, women crowded out onto the ladder, only to find its lowest section —which should have opened down onto the street—stuck in place. The upper parts of the fire escape became jammed with women unable to get down, while others pressed on them from the window above. Rushing to other windows, women cried and called for help, then finally, one after another, leaped from the building, with their clothes afire. Below one window stood an iron picket fence, and several women fell directly upon it, impaled on the pickets. A few who landed on the sidewalk survived, but many did not. And inside, trapped workers were charred beyond recognition.

Firemen had arrived quickly and fought bravely, and the fire chief was seriously injured when a part of a brick wall collapsed upon him. But all their efforts could not get four hundred women out in time. The Gottlieb family lost three daughters. Teresina Tartaglia left behind three small children. An elderly widow named Reynolds was never found. All together, twenty-five women died, and scores were injured. As crowds gathered to watch the firemen hosing down the

Fighting the fire at the Triangle Shirtwaist factory. Photograph courtesy of UNITE Archives, Kheel Center, Cornell University.

embers, they saw cards fluttering and scattering on the ground. They were from the paper-box company that had been inside the building, and they read "Merry Christmas."[19]

Four months later, on March 25, 1911, an even more deadly fire erupted in New York, in the center of the Garment District. This time, it happened in a large and modern building, supposedly fireproof. The fire started at 4:40 on a Saturday afternoon, and most of the workers had gone home hours before. But on the upper floors, the Triangle Shirtwaist Company girls were still at work. Triangle had refused to settle in the shirtwaist strike the year before, and so the employees had no Saturday half holiday. Six hundred workers filled the eighth, ninth, and tenth floors, and were locked into their workrooms. Some later said the doors were locked to keep the girls from slipping out into the stairwells for a break from their work; others said it was to keep them from stealing fabric and clothing. The company denied that the doors were locked at all.

Although the brick structure itself did not burn, the fire spread quickly among the workrooms, where the girls were surrounded by lint, scraps of cotton and linen, piles of shirtwaists, and wooden worktables. The lone fire escape melted and twisted, and the inside staircases—even had the doors been unlocked—could never have taken six hundred workers out in such a rush. The elevator made a few trips up and down before the fire stopped it, and on the tenth floor the workers—and the bosses—escaped out over the roof. But on the eighth and ninth floors, the women were trapped.[20] Some of them burned to death: their bodies were found pressed against the locked doors. Others, like the girls in Newark, jumped from the windows, but this time they were leaping from the eighth and ninth floors. Clearly they chose to die quickly from the fall rather than slowly from the fire and smoke. Their crushed and broken bodies remained on the sidewalk for hours as firefighters fought the flames. In the gutters of the street, water from the fire hoses ran red with blood.[21]

One hundred and forty-six women died on that day in March, and the city was horrified by the disaster. On a rainy day in April, 120,000 people marched in a funeral procession for the dead who could not be identified.[22]

Anne Morgan arranged for a mass meeting at the Metropolitan Opera House. It was partly a memorial, partly a fund-raiser, and partly an inaugural event for the Citizens' Committee on Safety. Every seat in the hall was filled. When it was Rose Schneiderman's time to speak, she addressed not the workers, but the allies, the reformers, the politicians. She had lost personal friends in the fire, but,

Memorial march after the Triangle Shirtwaist fire. Photograph courtesy of UNITE Archives, Kheel Center, Cornell University.

more important, she had realized just how little had been accomplished by the waistmakers' dramatic uprising only a year before. Tight with emotion, her voice, accustomed to ringing out over the clamor of street meetings, on this occasion nearly failed her. She could speak only above a whisper, but the crowd was so silent that they had no trouble hearing the tiny figure up on the stage.

> I would be a traitor to these poor burned bodies . . . if I came here to talk good fellowship. We have tried you good people of the public and we have found you wanting. The old Inquisition had its rack and its thumbscrews and its instruments of torture with iron teeth. We know

> what these things are today: the iron teeth are our necessities, the thumbscrews the high-powered and swift machinery close to which we must work, and the rack is here in the fire-proof structures that will destroy us the minute they catch on fire.
>
> This is not the first time girls have been burned alive in the city. Every week I must learn of the untimely death of one of my sister workers. Every year thousands of us are maimed. The life of men and women is so cheap and property is so sacred. There are so many of us for one job it matters little if 143 of us are burned to death.
>
> We have tried you, citizens; we are trying you now, and you have a couple of dollars for the sorrowing mothers and daughters and sisters by way of a charity gift. But every time the workers come out in the only way they know to protest against conditions which are unbearable, the strong hand of the law is allowed to press down heavily upon us. . . .
>
> I can't talk fellowship to you who are gathered here. Too much blood has been spilled. I know from my experience it is up to the working people to save themselves. The only way they can save themselves is by a strong working-class movement.[23]

Finally the garment makers of New York were heard. In Albany, Governor John A. Dix appointed a factory investigating commission, which collected fifteen thousand pages of data on working conditions around the state. Rose Schneiderman testified before the committee herself, and recruited other working women to speak as well.[24] The hearings removed whatever doubt may have remained in the public mind about the exploitation of working women. The state legislature then passed several new laws regulating safety and sanitary conditions, and in 1912 it limited the workweek to fifty-four hours for women in many factories.

The new law, however, was rarely enforced. In 1913, girls in candy factories still spent thirteen hours a day packing chocolates; in an ostrich feather shop, seventeen-year-olds worked from early morning until 9 P.M. three nights a week. In the canneries, where the new law did not apply, women worked as long as 119 hours a week during the harvest season. And youngsters in the white-goods trade were still working sixty hours a week, in spite of the fifty-four-hour law.[25]

The white-goods workers had watched the shirtwaist strike, and they were encouraged. They watched the Triangle fire and they knew that their own workplaces, in rundown wooden tenement buildings and basement sweatshops, were

Pushing bones into corsets. Women's Bureau photograph, courtesy of the National Archives at College Park (RG 86G-2B-1).

even more dangerous. Finally, they began to listen to Rose Schneiderman. She came back, again handing out circulars in front of factory doors and climbing onto her little ladder to speak. She asked them to come to meetings after work; she urged them to join the International Ladies Garment Workers Union. Her work was matched by Fannia Cohn, another Jewish immigrant—a middle-class woman who had chosen a life as a garment worker because of her commitment to the cause of workers. In her childhood in Poland, Cohn had absorbed a revolutionary fervor, and she passed it along to the young white-goods workers as she taught them English and the principles of trade unionism at the same time.[26]

Still, for all this effort, no more than three hundred women in the city's white-goods shops were ever organized at one time. With more than ten thousand white-goods workers in the city, and with constant turnover in the trade, a shop-by-shop campaign could never reach them all. The situation called for a dramatic and risky gesture—a general strike. If they could get all the white-goods workers to go out together, the unions could negotiate for them all at once. Leaders of both the Women's Trade Union League and the ILGWU resisted the idea, but Schneiderman and Cohn and their small corps of white-goods workers pushed forward.

Again they distributed handbills outside the factory doors, morning, noon, and night—this time calling a meeting for January 6, 1913, for all white-goods workers, asking them to come and vote on the question of a general strike. On the night of the meeting, Cooper Union was filled to overflowing, and a second meeting had to be convened at a nearby temple. The vote was unanimous. On Thursday morning, the white-goods workers would not go to work.

Instead they went to meeting halls set up in neighborhoods around the city. By the afternoon of the second day, seven thousand of them were on strike—American-born women and girls, as well as immigrants. One social worker described them as "the youngest, the most ignorant, the poorest and most unskilled group of women workers who ever went on strike in this country."[27] Fourteen- and fifteen-year-olds went out on picket duty like little soldiers, into the cold and snow of a New York City winter. Sometime during the day they would come back into the meeting halls for warmth and for food. Volunteers made sandwiches on thickly sliced bread, and served sympathy and encouragement along with hot coffee. By the time the strike was just a few days old, this lunch was the only meal many girls had each day. Some of them needed more help—a couple of dollars to pay the rent, perhaps. And the strike committee tried to answer the need, or the volunteers opened their own purses to keep a girl from starving or being evicted from her rented room.

Out on the street, the police and the hired guards again treated the strikers brutally. One officer, escorting a strikebreaker home, pushed a striker off a moving streetcar.[28] Another drew a gun on a small group of girls and threatened to shoot them. And again the mink brigade mobilized for their protection. Fola La Follette, an actress, feminist, and daughter of Senator Robert La Follette, visited the picket lines and the jails, creating headlines in the papers and, ultimately, convincing her father to sponsor an investigation.[29] Leonora O'Reilly, vice president of the WTUL, serving on picket duty, was arrested for calling out "Scab!" as strikebreakers came out of a factory building. The word "scab," a derogatory term for a strikebreaker, could be seen as a threat, and O'Reilly claimed that she had only cried "Shame, shame!" She and eight other picketers were nevertheless hauled off in the police wagon, singing the "*Marseillaise*" all the way to the station. Edna Kenton, a prosperous writer, was also on that picket line, but the police, seeing her fur coat, refused to arrest her along with the others.[30]

The striking white-goods workers were not always blameless in the conflicts with police. Especially during the early part of the strike, picketers occasionally attacked strikebreakers, punching, scratching, and pulling hair.[31] More often, the women were peaceable. When the Women's Trade Union League brought more than two dozen cases of false arrest before the police commissioner and charged officers with use of undue force, a number of policemen were removed or reprimanded.[32] But for the most part the young women simply had to endure the fines and imprisonment. Where companies had asked the court for special injunctions against picketing, even peaceably walking up and down the sidewalk could lead to arrest. When one worker justified her picketing with the claim that "this is a free country," the judge replied "the freedom of this country, young lady, will cost you $3.00."[33]

White-goods workers were not the only rebels in the winter of 1912–1913. The shirtwaist makers had walked out again, and so had men's tailors and workers in the kimono and wrapper industry. All together more than 150,000 New York City garment workers were on strike.[34]

Their cause got a further boost when Teddy Roosevelt showed up at one of the union halls. The former president—still a potent force in American politics—arrived by cab at a hall on Henry Street, where several hundred young kimono makers had gathered for the opportunity to meet him. With his hat

An underage worker carrying kimonos for finishing at home. The New York white-goods strikers of 1913 insisted on an end to the home work system in their trade. Photograph by Lewis Hine, courtesy of the National Archives at College Park (102-LH-2861).

tucked under his arm, Roosevelt strode in, smiling broadly and shaking hands all around, then leaned against a desk and raised his hand to call for silence. "Now, young ladies," he said, "I want to know all about your lives, how you work, and how you manage to be cheerful. Just gather around me and tell your stories." His request, translated into four languages, brought a rush of testimony—first from a sixteen-year-old Spanish girl who told him that she had been working for two years, from eight in the morning to nine at night, making thirty-six kimonos a day. Roosevelt's smile faded quickly as, one after another, the girls told about long hours and low wages, about paying the company for the use of the sewing machines, about not being allowed to sing while they worked, and about trying to support themselves and often their younger siblings on six or seven dollars a week. After two hours, the burly ex-president turned to the child welfare worker who had brought him to the meeting and pronounced his judgment: "This is crushing the future motherhood of the country. It must be stopped. It is too horrible for words." After visiting a second meeting hall, Roosevelt vowed to promote state legislation to protect the young factory workers.[35]

Amid all the publicity, union organizers still had to take care of the business of running the strikes. When the white-goods strike began to look like it might succeed, the men who had control of the International Ladies Garment Workers Union finally offered their support and took over some of the day-to-day business of coordinating the picket lines and providing relief to the workers. Rose Schneiderman, however, was still kept busy as chairman of the settlement committee organized to negotiate with the employers.

The manufacturers had formed their own organization to deal with the strike committee, and they soon agreed to most of the workers' demands: a standard fifty-hour week, extra pay for anything over fifty hours, an increase in wages with a minimum of five dollars per week, and an end to the practice of sending work out to sweatshops and home workers. But they refused to recognize the union or to guarantee that strikers could come back to work. They also resisted creating a "preferential shop," in which union members would be hired unless a nonunion member was better qualified. This last had been the critical component in the Protocol of Peace, negotiated by Louis Brandeis during the cloak makers' strike of 1910. Brandeis, at this point not yet a Supreme Court justice but a prominent attorney who took a great interest in the peaceful settlement of industrial conflicts, intervened again. Finally, when the strike was five weeks old, the manufacturers recognized the union and agreed to the preferential shop. Then, as Rose Schneiderman said, "the joy of the strikers was complete."[36]

New protocols in other cities improved conditions in the garment trades, but in many other industries labor unrest did nothing to improve conditions. And often in men's industries the strikes became especially bloody. In mining and lumber districts, companies facing a strike could hire private "labor adjusters" who boasted that they could put "10,000 armed men into the field inside of seventy-two hours."[37] As strikers met these private armies, the government was forced to intervene. Between 1894 and 1915, martial law was declared ten times in Colorado, on several occasions in Idaho, and at least once—during a coal strike—in West Virginia. Finally, late in 1913, Congress authorized, and

Woodrow Wilson appointed, a Commission on Industrial Relations "to inquire into the general conditions of labor . . . to discover the underlying causes of dissatisfaction in the industrial setting." After 154 days of hearings—running well into 1914—the commission itself would be torn apart by the divisions between business interests and labor interests. In the end, the commission submitted three dissenting reports. "Big" Bill Haywood of the Industrial Workers of the World called the commission "a tragic joke" and vowed that the struggle would go on, no matter what the commission or Congress might do.[38]

Even in the garment trades, the peace promised by the new protocols could not last. Late in 1913, the economy fell apart again. It was the third major collapse since 1907. The stock market crashed, banks failed, and businesses closed. President Wilson, who had pledged to reform the banking system, pushed the Owen-Glass Act through Congress, setting up the Federal Reserve System, which would eventually help stabilize the economy. But in California and Oregon in 1913, bands of unemployed men roamed from one town to another, seeking food or work, or even just some sort of public acknowledgment of their plight. In New York, it snowed all winter and was bitterly cold, and three hundred thousand were out of work. Men showed up at the employment offices with their feet wrapped up in rags. On January 12, 1914, the New York *Call* reported that local charities could not keep up with the needs of the unemployed: "A thousand hungry men and boys lined the Bowery in the cold early morning yesterday from the Bowery Mission to Houston Street. The line was ever increasing and hundreds were turned away when a bell, rung from the kitchen of the mission, announced that the supply of rolls and coffee had vanished."[39] On the night of February 13, with the temperature in the single digits and a fifty-mile-an-hour wind blowing out of the northwest, nearly two thousand homeless people—women, men, and children—spent the night on the steamboats and the Charities Pier on the East River. Others, who found no shelter, died on the street, and at least one baby died that night because he came uncovered in his crib in an unheated apartment.

That same day in Detroit, with the temperature below zero, eight thousand of the unemployed attempted to march in a demonstration. The radical Industrial Workers of the World (IWW) had begun organizing the unemployed, and their influence could be seen in the signs carried by the demonstrators. A man with long hair, wearing a gray overcoat, hoisted a sign that read "We Want Work—Not Charity, I.W.W." The other side of his sign posed the question "Bread or Revolution—Which?" Patrolmen and mounted officers wielding clubs and revolvers charged the demonstrators. They beat the man in the gray coat and routed the rest before the march could even begin.[40]

In March, more than twenty-five thousand silk workers were on strike in and around Paterson, New Jersey. Silk manufacturers, in an attempt to cut costs, had put each loom operator in charge of four looms. Led by the IWW, the workers demanded an end to the four-loom system and establishment of an eight-hour day—not just to ease the burden on each worker but to provide jobs for the unemployed. The strike lasted twenty-two weeks and achieved nothing. In August, the workers returned to their four looms, their ten-hour days, and their steamy workrooms.

In the West, conditions were no better. At the Colorado Fuel and Iron Company, striking workers evicted from their company-owned homes set up a tent city just off company property. When the local militia set fire to the tents, two women and thirteen children died. Enraged miners attacked the militia, and in the ensuing battle more than thirty men were killed.[41]

■

On June 28, 1914, Archduke Francis Ferdinand, heir apparent to the throne of Austria-Hungary, was assassinated by a Serbian radical. When Austria demanded apologies and reparations from the Serbian government, Russia supported Serbia's refusal to meet the punitive demands. Austria, supported by Germany, declared war on Serbia in late July, and then on Russia and France in early August. When the Austrians and Germans launched a campaign across Belgium, heading toward France, Great Britain entered the conflict. As Montenegro and Japan joined the Allies and the Ottoman Empire joined the Central Powers, America declared its neutrality. By November, the battling armies had reached a stalemate along the western front. Advancing and retreating in bloody trench warfare, the soldiers fought over a line that would remain essentially unchanged for the next three years.

■

Rose Schneiderman, now thirty-two years old, was as appalled as anyone in America by the war that had engulfed her native Poland. But she remained focused on her immediate goals. American working women must organize and, she had come to believe, they must also be allowed to vote. Women's unions were simply too weak, and most men's unions would not admit women. Even the American Federation of Labor, which claimed to support organization for women, was ineffective and essentially indifferent to women's unions. The gov-

At a suffrage rally on Wall Street in 1911, Rose Schneiderman addressed an audience of men—who, after all, were the only ones who could vote in favor of woman suffrage. Photograph courtesy of Rose Schneiderman Photograph Collection, Tamiment Institute Library, New York University.

ernment was slow to pass protective laws, and often the existing laws were not enforced. Only through the ballot, Schneiderman believed, could working women help shape their working conditions. And only as voting citizens could they achieve justice from the police and the courts. In December 1914, she traveled to Washington with a group of suffrage leaders for a meeting with Woodrow Wilson. She compared the workers' struggle in America with the violence in Europe: here, she said, there is "an industrial war going on." She described how workers had been starved and beaten in New York and Massachusetts. She cited the numbers killed and injured in industrial accidents, and described the Triangle fire. "The horrors in Belgium are more spectacular than they are here, perhaps," she told the president, but only in degree. Help women win the vote, she urged, and they would help end America's industrial warfare.[42]

Wilson was not yet ready to support women's voting rights; he would not be ready for two more years. And so Rose Schneiderman went back to her task among the garment workers, traveling to Cleveland, Chicago, and Philadelphia. In Springfield, Massachusetts, she set up a local branch of the ILGWU in a corset factory. In Worcester, she tried but failed to organize workers in a Warner

A knitting factory during the slack season. Women's Bureau photograph, courtesy of the National Archives at College Park (RG 86G-11A-4).

Brothers corset factory. In Boston, she helped shirtwaist makers win an agreement for a closed shop.

The work was especially difficult in a time of depression and unemployment. In the garment factories of New York, young immigrant women continued to report to work every day, but often there was nothing for them to do. And since they were paid by the piece, no work meant no pay. Lisa Hasanovitz, who had arrived alone from Russia in 1912 with eight dollars in her pocket, worried about the family she had left behind, who now suffered from both poverty and war: "Weeks wore on, and no orders came in. We were already tired out with the dulness, and with fear we met each new-coming day that brought us no work. Having nothing to do, we would gather in groups near our machines and tell our troubles—the main theme being the war. Nearly all had families or relations in either Poland, Lithuania, or Galicia, who were ruined by the war, and whom these girls had to help. Until now, they had deprived themselves of necessities and shared their scanty earnings with their unfortunate relatives, but now there was nothing they could share."[43] Worse yet, the price of food began to rise. In February 1915, the mayor of New York wrote to President Wilson, warning of the "prospect of much hardship and suffering." The price of bread, he claimed, had increased 20 percent over the period of a few days.

■

Britain had declared the North Sea a military zone and blockaded German ports. By March, the disruption of America's ability to trade in Europe had become painfully clear, and Wilson filed a protest of the blockade. The British did not back down.

■

In Seattle, the IWW was encouraging men to break into restaurants and take food. And in Philadelphia, the Home Relief Emergency Committee hung out a sign saying "no more applications received."[44]

CHAPTER THREE

From Corsets to Cartridges: Bridgeport, 1915-1916

SUDDENLY, IN THE EARLY MONTHS of 1915, the depression lifted. The warring nations of Europe needed arms and ammunition, and the United States—officially neutral—was free to supply both sides. Across the industrial North, factories began to order materials and buy equipment. Plants that had stood nearly idle began producing nails, rivets, nuts, and bolts to send overseas. Steel mills restoked their fires and built new furnaces; shipyards began to order lumber again; ammunition plants needed chemicals; railroads purchased track supplies; gun makers ordered lathes and milling machines.[1] And all of these industries, of course, needed workers. Since the onset of the war, however, the flood of immigration from Europe had essentially ceased. At Ellis Island, nearly as many people were leaving—heading east to fight in their homelands—as were arriving in America. And so in the American cities and towns where arms and ammunition were made, the desperate unemployment of 1914 became the labor shortage of 1915. At first the factory owners brought in men from other industries and other towns; but by summer employers began to see that the still gaping shortage of workers would have to be filled by women.

In Bridgeport, Connecticut, the labor shortage hit hard and fast. Seated on the sandy north shore of Long Island Sound, Bridgeport had a divided industrial heritage: it was near enough to the Connecticut River Valley to be bathed in that region's tradition of machine tool and gun making, but close enough to New York City to catch spillover from the garment trades. Within these two industries, labor followed the conventional division by gender. At Bryant Electric, the Remington Arms factory, and the Union Metallic Cartridge Company, men performed skilled work on machines or hazardous work with explosives. Most of the married women in town did not work for wages, their husbands being skilled mechanics with aspirations for the middle-class ideal of a wife free to tend her home and children. The women who did work for wages—roughly a third of them teenagers—were divided among sales, domestic service, office work, and the garment and textile industries. A few women had found their way into the metal trades, but very few.

Above all, for the women, Bridgeport was a center for white goods. The Warner Brothers Company, headed by De Ver H. Warner, a prominent local citizen, employed thousands of hand sewers and machine operators. Others found work at Crown Corset or at La Resista Corset Company.[2] Like the white-goods workers of New York, they worked a sixty-hour week, tacking on pink ribbons or stitching simple seams. In a large room filled with power sewing machines, the wheels whirred loudly and the wooden floor vibrated, while a hundred needles flashed up and down, driving through the fabric at the rate of one thousand stitches per minute.[3]

Within the garment companies, or in nearby factories, girls, boys, and women assembled paper boxes for packing the white goods. The wages here were even lower than in the corset workrooms, and young women were embarrassed to have it known that they were paper-box assemblers.[4] Standing all day at long tables in dusty rooms, with the strong smell of glue filling the air, the workers brushed paste on the cardboard and folded and shaped the boxes. They pasted on strips of muslin to reinforce the corners of each box. Then another group, stationed at cutting machines, trimmed off the ends of the muslin strips. This was the routine: hold the box in place; grasp it firmly so it cannot slip; press on a treadle to bring the blade down, and cut off the excess muslin; remove the box and quickly put another in place; then press the treadle again. Some of the

Paper-box worker. Photograph by Lewis Hine, courtesy of George Eastman House (GEH 5123).

machines had guards to keep a girl's fingers from getting too close to the blade. But the guards slowed down the pace, and a slower pace meant a smaller pay envelope at the end of the week. And so box makers often worked with the guards moved up out of the way. Then fingers were cut, or even cut off, in the relentless race to earn a few extra pennies by making an extra hundred boxes a day.[5] This was considered light, clean work, suitable for young women awaiting marriage. Girls who worked in department stores undoubtedly lost fewer fingers, but their wages were even lower, and they, too, had to stand all day.

Such was the work of the young women of Bridgeport in the spring of 1915, when the local makers of guns and ammunition began receiving orders from abroad. The American-British Company had an order for $2.5 million worth of shrapnel shells for Russia. The Locomobile Company was making 500 five-ton armored cars. Remington Arms needed a new plant to accommodate its $168 million in orders for small arms. Union Metallic Cartridge (UMC), recently merged with Remington, had enormous orders for ammunition. Any company that could make arms or ammunition, it seemed, had enough work lined up to keep busy at full capacity for two or three years.[6]

■

The Germans, to cut off British supply routes, began to concentrate on submarine warfare. On May 7, off the coast of Ireland, a German sub sank the British liner Lusitania, *killing nearly two thousand civilians, more than a hundred of them Americans. The ship had been unarmed, but was reportedly carrying munitions from America to the Allies. Suddenly, American feelings of neutrality began to evaporate. Although many called for an immediate declaration of war, Wilson chose diplomacy. He sent a message of protest to Germany, demanding both reparations and a promise not to sink passenger ships without warning. Germany at first refused even an apology.*

■

When the first large war orders came to Bridgeport, workmen began to arrive from around the country. Bridgeport, however, was utterly unprepared for the great rush of newcomers: there was simply no place to put them. Men who brought their families with them were forced to go home again, for lack of housing.[7] Men who came alone, leaving their families behind, crowded into boardinghouses.[8] By summer, twenty-five thousand newcomers had arrived, and there was talk of putting up a tent city for three hundred homeless families.[9] So rapid was the growth of business that enough men simply could not be found. Then a rumor began to circulate: women would be taken into the munitions plants, and their wages would surpass anything available in the women's trades.

And so women simply walked away from their sewing machines and their paper box tables. They left their clerking positions in the department stores of Bridgeport and nearby towns. Suddenly there was a shortage of domestic servants in New York City.[10] By midsummer, five thousand young women had begun working at the Remington Arms–Union Metallic Cartridge company alone.

The new work was no more complicated than the women's accustomed tasks. Long before the introduction of women into these industries, many jobs

Wrapping packages in a department store brought wages even lower than women's factory work. Photograph by Lewis Hine, courtesy of George Eastman House (GEH 37543).

had been mechanized and subdivided so that they could be done by unskilled or semiskilled immigrant men who had no leisure for training and little or no command of English. A woman who had stamped out buttons by machine could easily learn to draw out brass cartridges. A young girl who had inspected corsets could inspect or pack rifle shells, and a sewing machine operator could learn to run a wire winding machine. Even a fourteen-year-old box maker could fill cartridges with powder. Accustomed to earning six or eight dollars a week, young women suddenly had the chance to earn ten dollars a week at the cartridge factory or at Bryant Electric.

By July, the women of Bridgeport—and the men—began to discover their strength in a tight labor market. The first to flaunt their power were the machinists and toolmakers, but the women were not far behind. The designers and builders of machine tools, beginning in the mid-nineteenth century, had brought about the second industrial revolution, creating machines that produced interchangeable parts. With interchangeable parts, mass production became possible. From guns to sewing machines to bicycles and automobiles, the machine trades had brought new consumer goods within reach of the middle class. Behind all of this growth in the consumer culture were machinists—the high-tech workers of their day. The lords of the trade could design and build machines capable of cutting metal parts with accuracy as fine as one ten-thousandth of an inch. The mere mortals among them could operate, repair, and adjust a variety of lathes, drill presses, milling machines, planers, and boring machines. Although an unskilled operator could be taught to use a machine tool, a genuine machinist earned his rank only through a long apprenticeship, an understanding of mathematics, and a good deal of native wit. This elite group of craftsmen, organized into the International Association of Machinists (an affiliate of the AFL), had already achieved comfortable wages, clean and bright workrooms, and considerable job security. They still, however, worked a nine- or ten-hour day.

National leaders of the machinists' union, watching the frantic arms buildup in the spring of 1915, planned a campaign for an eight-hour day, and they chose to begin in Bridgeport.[11] On the eastern outskirts of the city, Remington Arms was building a 102-acre small arms plant. Thirteen interconnected, five-story buildings, constructed from 18 million bricks, had gone up in four months' time. Local newspapers called it "the largest arms plant in the world under one roof,"[12] and the owners planned to hire sixteen thousand new workers to fill it. Suddenly in mid-July, on the flimsy excuse of a dispute over union membership for a group of millwrights, officials of the International Association of Machinists arrived in Bridgeport and announced that they would call a general strike of all machinists in the city. If the machinists walked out, then within a few days machines that needed to be repaired or adjusted would stop functioning; cutting tools that broke would not be replaced. Within two weeks, the leaders predicted, all but the corset factories would be shut down.

The man in charge of the construction operation for Remington, Major Walter W. Penfield, had just retired from the Army's Ordnance Department, and he had his own theory about the cause of the trouble: "There is not a shadow of doubt," he said, "that this whole thing is the work of Germans or German sympathizers" trying to delay production of arms for the Allies.[13] Despite the bluster, Remington at the very first sign of trouble announced that all employees would, on the first of August, be switched from a ten-hour day to eight hours with no cut in pay.[14] The machinist leaders, nevertheless, vowed to proceed with their general strike as scheduled, and to stay out until all machine shops in Bridgeport had gone to an eight-hour day.

As the threat of a general strike hovered over the city, Catherine Hewitt, head of the Bridgeport Protective Association, began to worry about the five thousand women who worked at the Remington Arms–Union Metallic Cartridge plant. During a machinists' strike, they would surely be thrown out of work, and they had no union of their own to provide emotional or financial support during a strike. The Women's Trade Union League had no active branch in Bridgeport—no group of wealthy allies, no working women trained in efficient strike management. Hewitt appealed to the AFL to do something to keep the Bridgeport women from harm, but the response was feeble. The AFL did send in an organizer named Mary Scully,[15] but there was little time to build up a women's union from scratch. And there was no way to keep the women at UMC on the job if the men walked out.

As the level of tension in the city rose, a group of Portuguese workers attacked a Remington guard for no apparent reason and with no particular motive. The company responded by putting bright lights up around the plant. At the company offices, they boarded up the doors and erected a six-foot barbed wire fence.[16] For their part, the three hundred Remington guards soon made it known that they would go on strike along with the machinists rather than be caught up in any violence.

Finally, the day of the walkout arrived. At noon on July 20, officials of the

In the annealing process, shown here at the Union Metallic Cartridge plant in Bridgeport, parts are heated and then cooled slowly to make the metal ductile enough to be shaped. Photograph courtesy of the National Archives at College Park (RG 86, box 8, Signal Corps photo 28778).

ironworkers' and machinists' unions waited outside the Remington factory, along with dozens of reporters, hundreds of spectators, and most of Bridgeport's police force. The signal for the walkout was to be the noon whistle; but at noon the whistle blew, and nothing happened. No machinists—no one at all—emerged from the plant. Leaders of the ironworkers' and machinists' unions paced up and down outside the plant, looked at their watches, and wondered what had happened to their men. At one o'clock, still no one had come out. Inside, Major Penfield had met with the machinists, offering them a permanent eight-hour day and a one-dollar-a-day increase in wages. Then he had a meal brought in from the company restaurant and left the men alone to talk. A few minutes before one o'clock, the Remington machinists—ignoring the instructions from the International's leaders—voted not to strike.[17]

Meanwhile, at the company's sister plant, Union Metallic Cartridge, more than one hundred young women had answered the strike call. They were not machinists, but they walked out of the building with their hats on—a clear sign that they were not intending to return soon. The crowd outside the factory cheered, and the girls walked up and down in front of the factory, calling for the remaining workers to come out. No more did come out, but a company official soon appeared to talk with the demonstrators. If they returned quietly to work, they were told, the entire force of five thousand women would be given a raise that would come to about sixty-five cents more a day. Remington had already offered an eight-hour day to all of them, and so with this second offer the women went back inside, took off their hats, and got back to work.[18]

Around the city, only a few hundred men actually walked out, but the episode turned Bridgeport into an eight-hour town almost overnight. Across the Sound, in Brooklyn, the E. W. Bliss Company, which made torpedoes for the U.S. Navy, announced an eight-hour day within hours of the aborted strike in Bridgeport.

■

That same week, the United States moved further away from neutrality and closer to war, when President Wilson sent his third, and most strenuous, note to Germany in protest over the sinking of the Lusitania. *Insisting upon the principle of freedom of the seas, Wilson stated that "the Government of the United States will continue to contend for that freedom, from whatever quarter violated, without compromise and at any cost."*[19] *In August, the Germans sank another British liner, the* Arabic, *killing two Americans. More protests and threats from Wilson eventually brought about a German promise not to sink passenger ships. It seemed, for the time, that Wilson had kept America out of the war.*

■

Late in the summer, the women of Bridgeport showed that they could act without the machinists. In spite of the earlier strike, the Bryant Electric Company had kept its women on a ten-hour day and sixty-hour week. On August 20, the day after the sinking of the *Arabic*, five hundred women assemblers and a few men walked out. Because these were unskilled workers, not machinists, the company tried to ignore them. But when the rest of the workers—fifteen hundred in all—joined in, Bryant capitulated. The workers would have not only a basic forty-eight-hour week, but higher base wages, time and a half for overtime, and double time on Sundays.[20]

And what of the corset factories? They had little choice but to follow the trend. In November, De Ver H. Warner, of the Warner Brothers factory, told a reporter from the New York *World*, "We are producing in eight hours fully 95 per cent of the output we made in ten hours. Our girls report more promptly and keep more steadily at their work. The greatest difference is in the atmosphere of contentment in the factory. We would not go back to the old system if we could."[21] Of course, they couldn't. They had trouble enough just attracting workers on any terms. Over that winter, the Warner company ran double-column advertisements calling for six hundred workers:

GIRLS:

Here is good work—and steady.
Here is interesting work—and not dangerous.
Here is good pay—for hundreds more.
Here are clean, light rooms—well ventilated.
Here is a 48 hour week—at all times.
If the war stops we go on.
We Need Help!
Do You Want Good Work at Good Pay?

The ad then described "club rooms of the Seaside Institute" where employees, in the evenings, could take classes in gymnastics, embroidery, and English. The company offered a free library and the services of a trained nurse.[22] It was a seductive call, but the young women of Bridgeport were not listening. The Union Metallic Cartridge plant could run a much simpler ad:

200 GIRLS WANTED

Light pleasant factory work. Eight hour shop. Good pay.[23]

Everyone knew that "good pay" in the cartridge shop would be several dollars a week more than "good pay" at the corset factory.

The movement of women workers from corsets to cartridges naturally

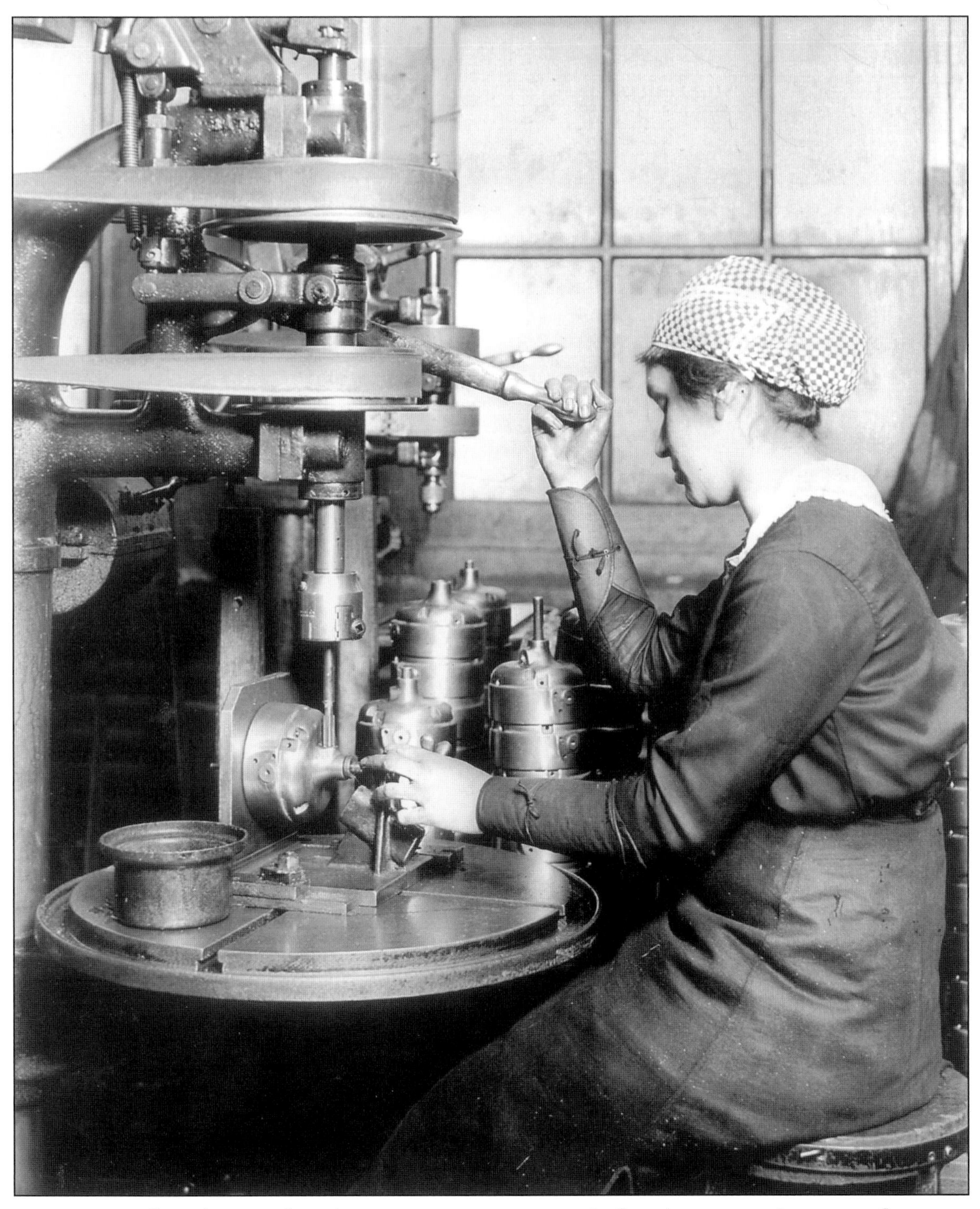

Caps, sleeve guards, and protective aprons were among the first adaptations to the presence of women in munitions factories. Women's Bureau photograph, courtesy of the National Archives at College Park (RG 86G-2F-8).

attracted the attention of social researchers. Amy Hewes, a professor of economics at Mount Holyoke College, arrived in Bridgeport and quickly set to work on a report that would be published by the Russell Sage Foundation, where Mary Van Kleeck was now heading up the Industrial Division. Hewes had been secretary of the Massachusetts Minimum Wage Commission and was rapidly becoming an acknowledged expert on the underpaid workers at the bottom of the economic order. She was also a charmer, a lover of life and of nature, a woman who made other people feel more alive.[24] If the women of Bridgeport were skeptical of her work at first, she quickly won them over. In typical Russell Sage style, Hewes visited the women workers in their homes, met their families, and got a close look into their lives. Her published report described a city under stress as it adapted to a wartime economy.

There were more American-born women in the Bridgeport industries than in the typical New York City factory. Still, Hewes found that more than half of the women either had been born in Europe or had parents born in Europe. A typical nineteen-year-old Jewish girl, unnamed in Hewes's report, told about her childhood in Russia. Her family had come across the Atlantic in steerage, along with thousands of others fleeing the repression of the czar's regime. After passing through Ellis Island, the family settled in New York, where the father struggled to make a living with some sort of pushcart business. The girl had managed to obtain a solid education, and instead of working in the garment trades, she was able to find a low-paying clerical job in the city. Sometime in 1915, she visited an aunt who lived in Bridgeport and there she discovered the boomtown opportunities. She took a job as an inspector of shells at UMC and urged the rest of her family to join her: there were jobs for everyone. When the family arrived, she was able to help her brother find a four-year apprenticeship at Remington Arms. Such apprenticeships, of course, were not available to young women, but the higher wages they could earn at UMC seemed enough for now.[25]

Helen, another nineteen-year-old, had worked in one of the novelty and paper box factories from the age of fourteen. She was an orphan, but was able to live with a friend, where she paid four dollars a week for room and board—a bargain, in her mind. But after four years of making paper boxes, Helen still earned only $7.50 a week. By the time Amy Hewes found her at UMC, Helen was making ten dollars a week inspecting shells. Though the work strained her eyes, she appreciated the wages and her working conditions. The foreman, she said, was particularly kind to girls who were alone and supporting themselves.[26]

Much of the work, Hewes found, was light and not particularly dangerous. Inspecting and packing shells called for speed, accuracy, dexterity, and attention to detail. Such work took no particular training and no more attention and care than any of the other work these young women had found. In the departments where the cartridges were actually made and filled, however, work took on a new kind of intensity.

The shop floor itself was different from a garment factory. The machines were larger and required more power than a sewing machine or a buttonholer or a grommet fastener. Somewhere within each long, brick factory building, an enormous steam engine drove the overhead shafting that ran the length of each room. Lined up under the shaft, fifty or seventy or a hundred machines might draw their power from one spinning iron flywheel. Leather belting connected the overhead shaft to the individual machines, each with its own gears and wheels turning at high speed. An overhead wooden stick allowed the operator to disengage her machine from the line shaft while she put her workpiece in place, then reengage with the spinning shaft. Except for those who had worked in textile mills, the women must have been astonished by the noise: the steady rumble of the line shafts, the slapping of leather belts, and the screech of tool-grade steel cutting or shaping softer metals.

The future cartridges came to the women as small brass cups, several boxes full arriving at one time. Placing the brass cups into hollow dies, the worker then passed them under a punch machine, which would draw out the brass into long, thin cylinders.[27] The work required close attention, and a moment's distraction could cause the machine to jam. Sometimes, a woman found that her machine overheated, and she had to stop to let it cool off. After the cartridges had been stretched to the right size and shape, another worker—on another machine—would trim them to make them all exactly the same length. The cartridges then moved on for "heading." At the heading machine, a woman fitted each cartridge with a small percussion cap, already filled with a powerful explosive—fulminate of mercury.[28]

Fulminate of mercury inflamed the women's eyes and sometimes left open sores on their skin. Sinks had been installed in the workrooms, but some foremen allowed the workers to wash only at the end of a shift.[29] That meant eight hours of handling chemicals with not even an apron for protection.[30] No one kept records on this industrial poisoning, but Amy Hewes was able to investigate the rate of injury from accidents. Once every week, on average, one woman was

Operating an internal thread milling machine at Norton Grinding Company in Worcester, Massachusetts. Photograph courtesy of the National Archives at College Park (RG 86G, box 8, Signal Corps photo 31653).

injured badly enough to miss ten or more days at work. Sometimes fingers were crushed in presses. That much might have happened in the traditional women's trades. But another day a big machine might overheat and send parts flying. Worst of all were the accidental explosions of gunpowder: "We always run," one worker told her, "but you never really have time to get away. It's all over before you know what's happened. It's just as if a big wind came and blew you across the room."[31]

Then there were the threats of sabotage. In February 1916, the rumor spread through Bridgeport that seven bombs had been found in one of the

In the early days at Union Metallic Cartridge in Bridgeport, the women wore no special protective clothing for filling hand grenades with powder. By the time this photo was taken for the Signal Corps in 1918 at Gorham Manufacturing Company, in Providence, womanalls had come into wide use. Courtesy of the National Archives at College Park (RG 86G, box 8, Signal Corps photo 31648).

Remington plants, supposedly put there by German spies or sympathizers. Company officials denied there were bombs and claimed that spies had spread that rumor to keep them from hiring more workers.[32]

A month later, just after seven o'clock on a snowy morning in late March, a loud explosion shook the UMC plant and startled everyone in the neighborhood. When the girls in the primer department heard the explosion, they rushed to the window. There, out in the yard, they saw a bleeding and mangled man, both his legs lacerated, his left side battered, and his left hand blown off almost to the wrist. A crowd of men rushed into the yard and an ambulance soon arrived to take the man, William Bergold, to the hospital, where the remainder of his hand was amputated at the wrist. The stress of the explosion proved too much for some of the young women. A few of them, according to the next morning's paper, became "hysterical and . . . were sent home for the day."[33] At the moment of the explosion, everyone probably thought first of the bomb rumors, but a quick survey of the yard made the true cause clear. Bergold had been carrying a two-pound box of explosives from a mixing shed into the main building. Apparently he slipped on the snow, and when the rubber box of fulminate hit the ground, it exploded. In this plant, any danger had more to do with lack of industrial safety than with sabotage. And yet the explosion reminded everyone that the war was coming closer to America.

■

In March, a German sub sank the French channel steamer Sussex, *and in April President Wilson threatened to break off diplomatic relations with Germany. Again, the Germans promised not to attack civilian ships without warning.*

■

Health and safety outside the shops also continued to trouble Bridgeport. While making the rounds of cheap rooming houses, the city health inspector, C. Howard Dunbar, found too many people sharing too few beds in small attic rooms with tiny windows, and he worried out loud about an increase in tuberculosis.[34] Family life and public morality also seemed threatened. The Board of Public Charities warned that the housing shortage—already causing the breakup of families—would soon lead to immorality and illegitimacy, as families took in excess boarders and as extended families filled small houses. Children whose parents could not care for them were being placed in orphanages; existing hos-

Making fuses at Gray and Davis in Cambridge, Massachusetts. Photograph courtesy of the National Archives at College Park (RG 86G, box 8, Signal Corps photo 31635).

pitals could not treat the increased number of patients; families who could not afford the rising rents were being evicted.[35] Thousands of women—young, single, and alone—had arrived to work in the factories and had no one to look after them. In short, officials and charity workers warned, the city was headed for disaster.

It was the YWCA that took the first practical steps in looking after the women. The "Y" established a housing referral service, which guided the girls to "reputable" houses. An expanded lunchroom provided inexpensive, fresh, nourishing meals served cafeteria-style. In the club's social room, the girls could read or play the piano. A gymnasium offered exercise programs, and in 1916 there would be talk of constructing a swimming pool. The YWCA aimed its programs at the girls who had left school at the age of twelve or fourteen and were thirsty for mental and physical stimulation. These girls also needed to be prepared for their assumed future roles as wives, mothers, and homemakers. Working all day at a machine that made one part of a rifle cartridge did little to equip a young woman for what she—and the community leaders and social workers—hoped would be her future life. And so, in the evenings, the Y offered classes in dressmaking, hat trimming, cooking, and furnishing a home on a small budget.

The city's leaders appreciated the YWCA's work, and more than once the local Vice Commission called upon Miss Upham, who headed the Y's local neighborhood outreach clubs, and asked her to explain to them what in the world was going on in the lives of the thousands of single young women in the factories—those mysterious creatures caught between childhood and adulthood. She dolefully explained to them that most of the girls spent their days in mindless, menial work. Outside of work they needed, and were bound to find, some sort of stimulation. Often, she said, they found it in "some movie or vaudeville show or cheap dance hall."[36]

At Poli's theater, a ticket to a vaudeville show could be had for ten cents. In April, Poli's advertised "the vivacious comedienne Eva La Rue in a Bright, Breezy Musical Comedy 'The Girl from Kokomo,' with the Popular Singing Ingenue Ruth Mitchell and a Bevy of Beauties Known as the Broadway Broilers." With tickets to the Ziegfeld Follies—also in town with the original New York cast—running between fifty cents and two dollars, we can only suppose that the young factory hands, both male and female, chose the vaudeville show over the elegant and more socially acceptable Ziegfeld. Another evening, another ten cents—a half-hour's pay—would buy a ticket to a movie described in the newspaper as "one of those screaming Keystone Comedies, 2,000 feet and a laugh in every foot."[37] When there was nothing to do in an overcrowded apartment at home—not even space to sit and entertain a guest—the ten-cent theater called strongly to restless young people. And a darkened theater filled with raucous, unchaperoned teenagers left most of the social reformers—and the city's vice commissioners—feeling quite uncomfortable. Miss Upham, the earnest YWCA leader, recommended more classes, more lectures and concerts, and better supervised dances.

Along with classes in homemaking, the YWCA tried to offer English classes to Hungarian and Polish immigrants, but could do little more for the newcomers. The Y simply did not have the money or the staff to develop enough programs. In all, the YWCA was able to serve only a few hundred of the thousands of young women in town.[38]

Finally, in April, the voters of Bridgeport passed a $2,275,000 bond issue for civic improvements. The money raised built fire and police departments in newly developed areas of the city. It created a new Health and Charities building, extended streets, constructed sewers, developed parks, and built schools.[39] A group of local businessmen formed a new housing company and began constructing homes.

Remington–UMC continued its own building program, putting up almost seven hundred houses for families and three large brick dormitories for single women.[40] For $1.75 a week, a woman worker could get a bed in an open dorm. For two dollars she could get a double room, and for three dollars a week she could have a private room. She also had use of the dormitory's quiet reading room, and of the reception room, where she could play the piano or entertain guests. The buildings offered modern cooking and laundry facilities, and shared—but modern—baths. In each of the three buildings, a matron had charge of offering maternal comfort and social discipline for 120 girls.[41] Compared to the cheap rented rooms in rundown sections of New York, the new Remington dormitories must have seemed quite elegant to the fortunate few who found lodging there.

The new dormitories got a good bit of press, but many of the working women in Bridgeport—young and old—still lived in family apartments. In the boomtown economy, prices went up nearly as fast as wages, and so unmarried girls were still helping out their parents, and wives of the lower-paid men still needed to work for wages. Amy Hewes found that in most families, three or more people had to work to pay the bills.[42] This meant father, mother, and the oldest among the children spent eight or more hours a day in the factories, while somehow keeping house and caring for younger children. Of the 5,000 women at UMC, about 370 were married, and a similar number had been married but were now widowed, deserted, or divorced. Hewes found many families, in fact, with no male wage earner at all.

For the women with children, vaudeville shows and cheap movie houses meant nothing, and there was no time for exercise classes, lectures, or self-improvement. On one of her home visits, Hewes interviewed thirty-three-year-old Susan Jones, who lived in a twenty-dollar-a-month apartment with her husband and four children. Susan had been born in England, and had started work there at the age of twelve. She had come to America in 1907, when her oldest daughter was a toddler and she was pregnant with her second child.

Through two more pregnancies, Susan worked in the men's clothing industry—probably sewing—for ten or twelve hours a day. Then, in the spring of 1916, she found work at the cartridge factory, in the annealing department. Now she was working only eight hours a day, with a short, six-and-a-half-hour day on Saturday. By this time, UMC had begun to run production around the clock, and Susan worked the second shift. She spent the morning tending to the housework and caring for her four-year-old while the other children were at school.[43] At three o'clock she reported to the factory, where she worked steadily until seven. Just before seven o'clock, outside the factory fence, there gathered a crowd of men and children, carrying packages of food. At seven Susan and the others hurried out to the fence to collect their dinners and say a quick hello, only to hurry back up to their machines, eat the simple meal, and begin work again—all within a fifteen-minute break. At eleven o'clock, these women would pour out into the night, to be replaced by a crew that would work until seven in the morning.[44]

Almost no one wanted the overnight shift; the younger women were especially uncomfortable traveling through the city to work at eleven at night. Occasionally, though, a worker claimed to prefer the night shift. One widow told Amy Hewes that the night shift allowed her to care for her four-year-old daughter during the day, and leave the child with her sister overnight. And on summer nights, she added, the factory was cool.[45] In another household, a woman and her widowed sister shared the care of the house and children, one working from seven in the morning until three in the afternoon, the other working from three until eleven at night. During a few rushed minutes at the factory gate at the change of shifts, they would share news and make plans for the family.[46]

■

While Europeans continued to grind at each other in the trenches of France, the United States remained caught in border skirmishes with Mexico. In June, the National Defense Act increased the size of the standing army to 175,000 and of the National Guard to 450,000. The U.S. Army faced its own need for arms and ammunition, but rumors of large domestic orders for munitions were hard to confirm.

■

While unskilled women worked in three shifts, Remington Arms put the skilled machinists back on two twelve-hour shifts because—in spite of the building boom—there were still too few houses and too few machinists in town. The

Even when women readily agreed to wear womanalls, they often refused to give up their stylish lightweight kid shoes. For recent European immigrants, especially, such shoes were an important sign of Americanization. Women's Bureau photograph, courtesy of the National Archives at College Park (RG 86G-8A-3).

machinists, evidently, were nevertheless satisfied, because they had established the principle of an eight-hour day at full pay, and were now receiving time-and-a-half for anything over eight hours.

For the women, who still had no effective labor organization, wages began to drift back downward by the following summer. "We used to get 12½ cents a thousand," said an inspector of shells at UMC, "and that certainly did make slick pay for a girl. But now they only give us nine cents for the same work."[47] In some jobs, the hours, too, began to creep back up beyond eight. Still, the wages in the corset factories and the departments stores could not compare. As long as the opportunity remained, women would move to new jobs, try new tasks, and struggle for higher pay.

When Amy Hewes wrote up her final report, *Women as Munition Makers,* she carefully documented the dangers of munitions work, the fatigue of the workers, the strain on families. Women on the overnight shift were falling asleep at their machines. Their young children, often cared for by only slightly older children, seemed "sickly and peevish." Long hours on the job created inefficiency, errors, and accidents. Hewes claimed that conditions in Bridgeport resembled working conditions in England during the first year of the war, before the government instituted protective reforms. "England," she wrote, "in her effort to manufacture huge quantities of munitions in a short time . . . went through a bitter industrial experience. She wore out her workers, created industrial confusion, lost the labor gains of years, and raised the unjust cry that British workmen were 'slackers.'"[48] In Bridgeport, according to Hewes, workers were being worn out even before the United States entered the war. America, she warned, must find some way to safeguard its workers, and thereby the health of the nation. Eventually, her colleague at the Russell Sage Foundation, Mary Van Kleeck, would be in a position to help protect these women.

■

The threat of entanglement in the European war would simply not go away. Britain published a blacklist of American firms that would be denied British trade because of their dealings with the Central Powers. A larger portion of American trade, however, was with the Allies themselves, and the Germans made their displeasure known with continued submarine threats to merchant vessels. The difficulty of remaining neutral became even more evident the day Black Tom Island blew up. At Black Tom, a manmade peninsula jutting out into the Hudson River behind the Statue of Liberty, munitions arrived by train to be transferred to ships heading for Britain. On July 30, 1916, two huge explosions obliterated the peninsula, raining molten metal on the Statue of Liberty, and blowing out windows in Brooklyn, Manhattan, and Jersey City. The exact cause of the explosions remained a mystery, but few doubted it was the work of German saboteurs.[49]

■

While Amy Hewes advocated government action, workers fought to protect their own interests. Food prices were climbing: bread had gone from five cents a loaf to six, and eggs were three cents a dozen. By fall, potatoes would be 75 percent above their prewar cost.[50] Through the spring and summer, strikes continued across the industrial North. In Ansonia, Connecticut, 4,500 employees struck against brass mills that supplied Remington–UMC, demanding a fifty-five-hour week at sixty hours' pay. Unskilled workers—speaking a dozen European languages—mobbed the plants to clear out any workers still on the job. When Joseph Ettor and Elizabeth Gurley Flynn of the radical IWW were reported to be on the way to Ansonia, warrants were filed for their arrest and guards were posted at the train station to catch them on their way into town.[51] In Hastings-on-Hudson, a girl in a green bonnet led a crowd of two hundred picketing the National Conduit and Cable Company. A bridge over the railroad tracks led to the factory, and the crowd of strikers occupied the bridge until National Guardsmen wielding bayonets drove them off.[52] At Westinghouse Electric in Pittsburgh, thirteen thousand workers—three thousand of them women—struck for a wage increase and an eight-hour day. When local police arrested two of those strikers for disorderly conduct, a crowd of five hundred, led by a drum corps, marched to the police station and occupied it, announcing that they would not tolerate the arrest of picketers.[53] Finally, the governor of Pennsylvania sent in one thousand National Guard troops to occupy the plant, and the strike was defeated.[54] Coal miners in the Pittsburgh area also went out on strike, and in Wilkes-Barre the United Mine Workers and the IWW faced each other in a pitched battle for control of the mines. On Long Island, an engineers' strike prevented tugboats from taking ships out to sea, and a boat loaded for London couldn't sail because its crew demanded 25 percent "war risk money."[55]

■

On October 8, 1916, German submarines sank six merchant steamships off Nantucket.

■

When the Commission on Industrial Relations published its three contradictory reports, it warned that industrial conflict—"a matter of the most serious moment during times of peace"—would become even more dangerous in time of war.[56] The members of the commission, unable to agree on their own conclusions, could not recommend any viable solutions; but the commission had served to bring the dangers of class warfare before the Congress and the country.[57] Meanwhile, the relationship between workers and employers could not help being changed by the labor shortage and the rapid growth in munitions industries.

The basic workweek, if not actual hours worked, had slid downward. The unions were gaining power and recognition. And as women moved into new jobs, researchers and reformers began to point out the dangers of the industries that had for the first time begun hiring women. In the eyes of the reformers and the union leaders, the European conflict created a chance to transform the lives of American industrial workers. For the working women themselves, in 1915, the opportunities of war work brought extraordinary new opportunities in their continuing struggle to make a living wage.

Meanwhile, in the South, a different sort of upheaval had begun.

CHAPTER FOUR

The Great Migration: Chicago, 1917

"MY DEAR SISTER, . . . THE PEOPLE are rushing here by the thousands and I know if you come and rent a big house you can get all the roomers you want. . . . When you fully decide to come write me and let me know what day you expect to leave and over what road and if I don't meet you I will have some one ther[e] to meet you and look after you. I will send you a paper as soon as one come along. [T]hey send out extras two and three times a day."[1] So wrote a woman who had just moved to Chicago, sending encouragement to family and friends in the South, adding her own very practical help to the seductive call of the newspaper that she promised to send.

That paper—the Chicago *Defender*—could not have been published in the South. In Memphis, when Ida B. Wells wrote editorials denouncing lynching, her newspaper office was destroyed and she was driven out of town. But in Chicago Robert Abbott and his staff felt safe. A transplanted Georgian, Abbott had established the *Defender* in 1905 and immediately had begun a crusade against the treatment of blacks in the South. The *Defender*—sent by mail and carried by black Pullman porters to thousands of people all across the southern states—did not just condemn lynching; it did not simply criticize the Jim Crow system of rigid segregation. When the wartime labor shortage hit northern industries, it urged blacks to leave the South in a mass migration: "The *Defender* invites all to come north. . . . Plenty of work. For those who will not work, the jails will take care of you. . . . Anywhere in God's country is better than the southland. . . . Come join the ranks of the free. Cast the yoke from around your neck. See the light. When you have crossed the Ohio river, breathe the fresh air and say, 'Why didn't I come before?' "[2]

They hadn't come before because they had not been welcome, and because there had been no jobs. Before the outbreak of the war, European immigrants arrived at Ellis Island, every year, in numbers roughly equal to the total number

A few nonwhite agricultural workers had made their way north by 1911, when this photograph was taken in Rochester, Massachusetts. Photograph by Lewis Hine, courtesy of the National Archives at College Park (102-LH-2542).

Large cotton planters hired "riders," who traveled from one farm to another to make sure that all available hands were busy in the fields. Women's Bureau photograph, courtesy of the National Archives at College Park (RG 86G-1B-1).

of African Americans living in the North.[3] Now, with immigration from Europe cut off and demand for American food and ammunition soaring, employers in the North, for the first time, welcomed labor from the South.

First, tobacco planters in southern New England recruited southern blacks to replace the Poles, Czechs, and Lithuanians who had been gathering and processing their crops. Then the Pennsylvania and Erie Railroads picked up trainloads of black men from cities in Florida, offering them not only jobs on the railroad but free transportation to Pennsylvania. Thousands of men accepted the offer, but then quickly scattered when they found better paying jobs in other industries. Then the railroads would bring up a thousand more.[4] Soon the wives and children of the men were coming north, too. And so, in 1916, the Great Migration had begun.

The new lure of northern jobs coincided with catastrophe in the South. For years southern sharecroppers had harvested and sold their crops, paid off their debts to the landowner and the plantation commissary, and then bought seed for the next year on credit. They seldom saw any cash, and often the only escape from a poor piece of land or an ornery landlord was to move to a different farm and start sharecropping again. Black women worked in the fields right alongside their men, and then did not only their own housework but that of surrounding white families. One Mississippi man reported that "after the summer crops were all in, any of the white people could send for any Negro woman to come and do the family washing at 75¢ to $1.00 a day. . . . They were never allowed to stay at home as long as they were able to go."[5] The young men, meanwhile, might go off to the sawmills through the winter months, leaving the women and older men to care for the livestock and keep things going until spring. Then early in the new year, when the northern states were still frozen over, southern farmers would plant the next crop, already mortgaged by large debts at the plantation store.

Into this difficult life marched the boll weevil. It had arrived from Mexico at the turn of the century and made its way across Texas, Oklahoma, Louisiana, and Arkansas. By 1913, weevils had reached Missouri; by 1915 they had crossed the Mississippi River and were destroying cotton crops in southeastern Alabama. Then, in the summers of 1915 and 1916, great floods across the central southern states washed away whatever cotton the hungry boll weevils had missed. With the crops destroyed, the planters lost money, no one had any credit, and many sharecroppers were driven off their farms. Letters to the *Defender* describe farm laborers with no way to start a new crop and often no land to plant even if they could come up with seed and supplies. "Wages is so low and grocery is so high until all I can do is to live. Please answer soon,"[6] one reader pleaded.

■

On January 31, 1917, Germany notified the United States that it would resume unrestricted submarine attacks on ships in the European war zone. In early February, a German sub sank the American steamer Housatonic. *The United States responded by breaking off diplomatic relations with the German government and by beginning to arm merchant ships.*

■

Not all southern blacks were sharecroppers. Women who were widowed or abandoned and could no longer make a living off the land often migrated to southern cities to find work. Married women, too, worked in far greater numbers than did married white women.[7] Whether single, widowed, or married, black women most often found work cooking, cleaning, and doing laundry, either in middle-class white homes or in restaurants and hotels. Small numbers of black women—about eighty-five hundred in 1910—worked for tobacco companies, sorting the large, rough leaves, stripping off stems, tying and twisting the leaves on frames for drying.[8] Black women had always shelled peanuts in the South, and as peanut growing became industrialized, they did the work at large production centers, sitting on benches or boxes in rustic sheds, getting up only to haul the heavy bags of peanuts to and from their benches. In coastal

Shucking oysters in Bluffton, South Carolina. Photograph by Lewis Hine, courtesy of the Library of Congress (LC-US-Z62-122661 [233373]).

towns, they shucked oysters or picked shrimp, generally preferring even such messy work to the long hours expected of domestic servants. A job that ended at sundown left a woman free to go home and care for her own family.[9]

Some southern black men had also given up farming, but they felt no more free or content than the sharecroppers who were trapped on the land. Young men who worked in sawmills or mines, like the sharecroppers, racked up heavy debts at company-owned stores. Miners who tried to abandon their jobs found that employers—aided by local sheriffs—would hunt them down and force them to return to the mine.[10] A few southern black men had become skilled craftsmen or small business owners, just as a some black women had become schoolteachers. But even with an education or a trade, their opportunities were limited by race. Then, as unions grew in the South, skilled black men were pushed out of bricklaying, blacksmithing, and carpentry.[11] When the cotton crops failed in 1915 and 1916 and penniless sharecroppers moved into southern cities, wages there dropped and many people could find no work at all.

Except in the tobacco and peanut industries, most factories were closed to black women and men alike. In South Carolina textile factories, it was illegal for blacks and whites to work together in the same room, use the same toilet, or even enter and exit through the same door at the same time.[12] When blacks did get into factories, they were invariably paid lower wages than whites. Blacks in the South—like the newest European immigrants of the North—struggled simply to survive.

Worse yet, African Americans had little protection against casual cruelty and mob violence. The *Defender* exposed these injustices in sensational language, without mercy for the white South: a black woman hung by a mob of twelve white men for the crime of slapping a white child,[13] black men routinely lynched for the alleged rape of white women. Southern blacks then wrote letters back to the editor, confirming the reports and begging for help finding jobs, in order that the writer might, in the words of one "willen workin woman," escape "this land of sufring."[14]

Alongside these indictments of the South, the *Defender* described life in the northern cities. It ran articles on movie theaters and nightclubs that were open to black audiences; it reported the exploits of black athletes; it printed advertisements offering what seemed like a week's wages for a single day's labor. The *Defender* described a world where black men could vote, where black children could go to integrated schools, and where a black woman could sit anywhere she found a seat on a streetcar, or could go into a shop and try on a hat and not be forced to buy it. The paper had a circulation of only 125,000,[15] but each copy was read and reread, passed around until it was worn out,[16] then saved as a relic by old men and women who had been slaves and had never learned to read.

Southern whites were trooping northward, as well, but no one seemed to notice their departure from the South, and once in the North they melted

Letters and postcards sent home by the early migrants encouraged others to follow. Here, three women posing with a studio prop automobile show off their city clothes. Photograph courtesy of the Library of Congress, Nannie Helen Burroughs Collection (LC-US-Z62-112102 [229893]).

In a cooking class at the National Training School for Women and Girls in Washington, D.C., black women were trained for work in modern urban kitchens. Photograph courtesy of the Library of Congress (LC-US-Z62-092635).

quickly into the white neighborhoods and the white workforce. The disappearance, however, of thousands of African Americans, the lowest paid of the southern workforce, quickly seemed like a crisis. Almost as soon as the movement north began, southern employers and plantation owners tried to stop it. First, city governments began confiscating the *Defender* before it could be sold, so that black Pullman porters and shopkeepers had to hide it in bundles of other goods.[17] From Lutcher, Louisiana, a man wrote asking about work, claiming that he could bring thirty or forty others with him. "Please don't publish this," he wrote, "because we have to whisper this around among our selves because the white folks are angry now because the negroes are going north."[18]

In Alabama, Arkansas, Mississippi, and Georgia, new laws restricted the work of northern labor agents and imposed exorbitant license fees.[19] On March 24, 1917, the *Defender* reported that a white labor agent named Kelly had been arrested at a train station in Brookhaven, Mississippi, where he had two carloads of men ready to head north. In Savannah the same day, according to the *Defender*, crowds attempting to buy train tickets were driven off by the police, who beat them with clubs and broke open their suitcases.[20]

None of these measures worked; the migration was under way. When blacks arrived in the North, there was of course never enough housing, and the railroads that had brought workers north sheltered many of them in tents and boxcars.[21] During the first winter of the migration, many died of exposure,[22] others of disease; but when the white southern press tried to frighten potential migrants, the *Defender* cited reports of African Americans freezing to death in the South, as well: "If you can freeze to death in the North and be free, why freeze to death in the South and be a slave, where your mother, sister and daughter are raped and burned at the stake; where your father, brother and sons are treated with contempt and hung to a pole, riddled with bullets at the least mention that he does not like the way he is treated. Come North then, all you folks, both good and bad. If you don't behave yourselves up here, the jails will certainly make you wish you had. For the hard-working man there is plenty of work—if you really want it. The *Defender* says come." [23]

And come they did. In the southeast, they headed for Philadelphia and New York; in the central south, they went to East St. Louis, Chicago, and Detroit. Some simply put down their tools and hopped a train. Others spent months preparing. Sometimes the men went ahead and found jobs before sending for the wives and children. Shopkeepers sold off their stock at a loss, boarded up the store, and moved the entire family at once. Preachers followed their congregations.

Many would-be migrants wrote letters back to the *Defender*, or to its advertisers, asking for railroad passes or for information about jobs. A widow with two daughters wrote asking for help finding a job as a cook. Another woman wrote to offer her services as "a body servant or nice house maid. My hair is black and my eyes are black and smooth skin and clear and brown, good teeth and strong and good health and my weight is 136 lb."[24] And from a seventeen-year-old girl:

"I can wash dishes, wash iron nursing work in groceries and dry good stores. Just any of these I can do. Sir, who so ever you get the job from please tell them to send me a ticket and I will pay them."[25] Another, a fifteen-year-old, wrote "I wont to come there and work i have ben looking for work here for three months and cand find any . . . i can do any work that come to my hand to do. . . . sin me a pass and you wont be sorry of it . . . i will work and pay for my pass if you sin it."[26]

Relatively few migrants actually had their fare paid by labor agents. More often, they had to get to the North on their own. Some formed clubs to get a group rate; others sold a house or their farm animals; some simply rode on freight cars.[27] All together, during the war, about half a million southern blacks would migrate to the northern cities; of those, about fifty thousand went through Chicago. Some then moved on to Gary and Rockford and Detroit, but many of them stayed in Chicago, settling on the South Side.[28]

They arrived at the train station in Chicago in their overalls and house dresses, hair wrapped in dust caps, sometimes bringing along chickens and pigs and goats. Met at the station by family or old neighbors from home, or by a volunteer from the Travelers' Aid society, they soon found their way to South State Street, the heart of Chicago's Black Belt. Nothing in the *Defender* or in letters sent home by earlier migrants could really have prepared them for what they found in the only part of the city that was open to them—the old vice district, where police left the gambling houses and prostitutes alone, as long as the only nearby residents were black.

In the words of the poet Langston Hughes, who visited Chicago during the war, "South State Street was in its glory then, a teeming Negro street with crowded theaters, restaurants, and cabarets. And excitement from noon to noon. Midnight was like day. The street was full of workers and gamblers, prostitutes and pimps, church folks and sinners. The tenements on either side were very congested. For neither love nor money could you find a decent place to live."[29] Stepping off a train into this dizzying new world, the immigrants needed, first, shelter, then work. Single young women might, if they were lucky, find that the Travelers' Aid volunteer directed them to the Phyllis Wheatley Home.

The home had been founded some years before by prominent club women, led by Elizabeth Lindsay Davis. Driven by a need to overcome racial stereotypes and by strong sense of duty, middle-class black women had long joined together into clubs that worked for "race uplift." Studying the classics, organizing charity balls, debating the proper role of "the Negro" in industry, encouraging the young people to practice oratory, or simply playing cards and sipping tea, the club women strove to overcome race prejudice by achieving gentility. The most important of the clubs, however, worked directly for the benefit of those who still struggled to survive.

The Phyllis Wheatley Club, named after America's first black female poet (who actually spelled her first name Phillis), had engaged in all of these uplifting activities, but in 1908 Elizabeth Lindsay Davis and Lulu Farmer began to worry about the single young women who were arriving in Chicago, without friends or family to guide and protect them. Should they not be offered the same kinds of support that the settlement houses and YWCA were offering to white girls? Otherwise, Davis and Farmer believed, they would go "astray by being led unawares into disreputable homes, entertainment and employment."[30] And so the club bought a nine-room, two-story house and founded the Phyllis Wheatley Home. It could house only twelve young women at a time, but could provide advice and social activities for other young women of the neighborhood as well. After 1908, the women of the Phyllis Wheatley Club focused most of their energy on the home. They sponsored dances and raffles to raise money for their work. From the Gaudeamus Club they received a donation of a dozen pillow cases. Mrs. Eva Johnson provided a ton of coal one winter. Dr. Fannie Emanuel visited the home and started a fund-raising drive by laying out five feet of pennies toward a goal of collecting a full mile of pennies for the home.[31]

Then the war came, and the trickle of migration turned to a flood. In 1915, the Phyllis Wheatley Home moved to a new building, which could house forty young women at one time. The new residents received not only food and shelter, but a crash course in urban living. For those who had been raised in log cabins, carried pails of water from the creek, and cooked over wood fires, life at the Phyllis Wheatley Home helped prepare for a probable future as domestic servants. Through cooperative living in a modern, two-story house, they learned about middle-class standards of cleanliness and modern methods of housekeeping.[32]

A house that could shelter only forty women at one time provided, of course, only one thread in the city's safety net. The year the Phyllis Wheatley Home moved to larger quarters, the women of the African American Club opened a YWCA for the black community. There, a few more young women could find rooms, and many more found a directory of "safe" homes for single girls, along with an employment agency and guidance on staying safe and healthy in the city. Later there would be other homes, including residences for single working mothers with children. Informally, black women opened their own homes to friends and relatives; they took in boarders; they provided warm clothes to the newcomers, nursed them through illness, and fed them when they were hungry.[33]

Help also came through the Chicago branch of the Urban League—then called the National League on Urban Conditions Among Negroes. Founded jointly by black and white citizens and aided by publicity in the *Defender*, the Urban League held its organizational meeting in Chicago in December 1916. Black women who attended the meeting included not only Elizabeth Lindsay Davis, but also Jennie Lawrence of the Phyllis Wheatley Home, Joanna Snowden-Porter of the Chicago Federation of Colored Women's Clubs, and Irene Sappington Goines—one of the few blacks in the Women's Trade Union League.[34] The Urban League would serve as a coordinating agency for the multitude of black self-help organizations, but it would also directly provide employment assistance. Its organizers planned to open their office before spring, and that would be none too soon.

In February 1917, the *Defender* began to announce a "Great Northern Drive" set to take place beginning on May 15, bringing a new surge of African Americans up from the South. Although no one was actually organizing such a drive, the mere publicity would make it happen. By March, when migrants arrived at the train station, a Travelers' Aid volunteer directed them to the offices of the Urban League and handed them a little card offering advice on making a smooth transition to Chicago life. Ten thousand of those cards were handed out the first year, and the Chicago club women, working with the league, visited two thousand newcomers in their homes. The Urban League held public meetings where speakers urged the migrants to become orderly citizens, efficient workers, and good housekeepers.[35]

■

On the first of March, the American public learned of a proposed alliance between Germany and Mexico, aimed at weakening the United States. Then, later in the month, the imperial Russian government—which was allied with France and Britain—was overthrown by mutinous troops. With the czar gone and the Provisional Government announcing political reforms, Americans suddenly found it easier to believe that the Allies were indeed fighting to overthrow totalitarianism.

■

As black migration increased, the Urban League and the club women scrambled to find housing and jobs for the newcomers. The Thomas family[36] came to Chicago from Seals, Alabama, and could find nowhere to live but a five-room apartment without electricity or gas or indoor plumbing. Of course, they had enjoyed none of these comforts as sharecroppers in Alabama, either, and their greatest need was to find work. Mr. and Mrs. Thomas were both illiterate, and Mrs. Thomas was uncomfortable with the bustle of the city, and self-conscious about her country clothes and country manners. While her husband and son found jobs in the stockyards, she took in laundry to earn a few dollars a week and stayed home as much as possible. Eventually the club women drew her out, for the urge to form social, charitable, and religious clubs extended to all levels of the black community.[37] After some months, she began to form connections and join clubs and feel comfortable in the city.

The Thomases also had a daughter, nineteen years old, who went out to work in a commercial laundry. Every day, the great city hotels, the restaurants, and the railroads produced wagonloads of linens in need of cleaning. Large laundry companies sent drivers around the city and out to the train stations, gathering the linens and bringing them to central plants, where laundry work was mechanized. For years, the hottest, heaviest work in these laundries had been done by white immigrant women, until the sudden labor shortage pulled those women into war industries. Now, in 1917, the Urban League sent black women to fill their places. They removed the wet sheets, towels, and tablecloths from the washers, shaking and untwisting them to prepare them for the mangles. The mangle operators, standing on wooden platforms over wet floors, fed the unwieldy linens into enormous steam-heated rollers, where the pieces wound their way through to come out flat and dry at the other end.[38] During the war, a few black women found jobs as checkers and sorters of linens, but mostly this lighter work was reserved for the remaining white women, working in separate rooms at higher wages.

In spite of the heavy work, young Miss Thomas and other black women far preferred commercial laundry positions to the more plentiful jobs in private domestic service, where they were often expected to work twelve hours a day, six and a half days a week. Working at a commercial laundry, Miss Thomas had her evenings free. She went to night school, and she sampled the parks, ice cream parlors, and theaters, which she had only dreamed of when the family worked as

Inside a commercial laundry in Virginia, around 1899. Photograph courtesy of the Library of Congress (LC-US-Z62-11803).

sharecroppers in Alabama. Most important, she and her family enjoyed the independence and anonymity of the city: they "were not noticed enough to be mistreated" by the white people around them.[39] There were limits—severe limits—to where they could live, and even limits to where her brother could walk without risk of being beaten by white gangs. But on the streetcars and in the stores and theaters and schools, many southern blacks for the first time felt free.

■

On March 18, German torpedoes sank three American ships, causing heavy loss of life.

■

Finding a job as a domestic or as a laundry worker was easy. Moving into factory work took patience, luck, or a willingness to work as a strikebreaker. Early in 1917, the International Ladies Garment Workers Union called a strike, and some of the employers hired several hundred black girls and women as strikebreakers. Transplanted southern farmers, uninitiated in the ways of worker solidarity, needed no persuasion to step into jobs abandoned by strikers. Even northern black workers were skeptical of the union's motives, because they had too often been excluded from membership, too often asked to join only when

Cutting and twisting wire for bedsprings. Women's Bureau photograph, courtesy of the National Archive at College Park (RG 86G 5L-2).

unions wanted to strike. So although the Urban League tried not to allow their people to be used as strikebreakers, employers had no trouble finding black workers to keep the factories going during a walkout. After ten weeks, with the union in disarray, the ILGWU called off the strike.[40] But the union had learned from this failure and immediately began recruiting the black workers as members, without discrimination against those who had come in as strikebreakers. In a short time they had even elected some African Americans to chair the shop committees. The ILGWU gradually rebuilt, and a year later would be able to pressure employers for concessions.[41]

■

On April 2, President Wilson delivered his war message to Congress. The German submarine warfare, he claimed, was "a war against all nations." He advised the Congress to "formally accept the status of belligerent which has been thrust upon it." Neutrality was no longer feasible while autocratic governments could menace the peace and freedom of other nations. "The world must be made safe for democracy," he insisted. Four days later, Congress passed a joint resolution declaring war on Germany.

■

As the date set for the Great Northern Drive approached, letters arrived at the *Defender* saying, "we are getting ready." In early May 1917, a black man was lynched in Memphis, and the following Saturday, according to the *Defender*, 1,200 Memphis blacks boarded a train to Chicago. On May 16, a reader from Mississippi wrote to the editors that "our pepel . . . are being snatched off the trains here in Greenville and a rested but in spite of all this, they are leaving every day and every night 100 or more is expecting to leave this week."[42] Crowded trains arrived in northern cities all through the following week. The timing of the Great Northern Drive had, by coincidence, been perfect. With the United States now in the war, the need for labor in American industry could only increase.

If an army travels on its stomach, then in 1917 meatpacking became a war industry. In the first years of the European war, demand for American meat products had immediately gone up. In 1916 alone, American meat packers had exported 70 million tons of canned beef, more than 260 million tons of fresh beef, and half a billion pounds of bacon to feed the soldiers and the hungry civilians of the warring nations.[43] Now they would have to feed the American armies as well. Packinghouses began by transferring workers from their southern plants

Weighing wire coils and recording the weights required both heavy lifting and some clerical ability. Women's Bureau photograph, courtesy of the National Archives at College Park (RG 86G-5L-1).

Few black women found such clean work in the canneries and meatpacking plants. War Department photograph, courtesy of the National Archives at College Park (RG 165-WW-587-5).

to the higher volume northern plants. Then they advertised in the *Defender*, hired labor agents, and offered transportation to bring workers north.[44] By 1917, more than ten thousand African Americans had found work in the packing plants of Chicago, and three thousand of them were women.[45]

Like other industries, meatpacking had been broken down into assembly line—or *dis*assembly line—procedures, speeding up meat production while reducing the need for skilled butchers. And as in other industries, black women did the dirtiest, wettest, smelliest jobs.

Melvina worked primarily in the fat washing department at the Morris and Company packing plant. A widow supporting a ten-year-old child and a ninety-five-year-old mother, she had arrived in Chicago in March of 1917, just ahead of the Great Northern Drive. Sometime after Melvina began work, the last men disappeared from the fat-washing room and the work was entirely taken over by women. For twenty cents an hour, she stood all day in front of a tub, washing fat under sprinklers—first under cold water, then hot, her hands under water all day.

In other parts of the packing plants, black women split open hogs' heads and removed the brains. They cut the ear drums and trimmed the snouts and tongues. In the casing room, they stripped fat from the outside of the intestines and scraped mucus from the inside, then turned the casings by forcing water through them. They measured and inspected the casings that would later be stuffed with sausage meat. At some stages, the meat had to be kept chilled, and the women worked in heavy dresses, sweaters, and shawls. Other rooms were hot. Under low ceilings, in windowless rooms lit only by bare electric bulbs, temperatures reached 115 degrees Fahrenheit in summer.[46]

■

During two weeks in April, the French army lost almost as many men as the entire active force of the U.S. Army. As Congress debated enacting a selective service system, the first six U.S. destroyers left Boston for Ireland, where they took up escort duty and antisubmarine patrol.

■

As more men disappeared from the packing plant, Melvina's work expanded. She began to spend her mornings in a basement room cutting meat for sausages—taking the fat and meat off pig tails, and cutting meat off neck and rib bones. Then in the afternoons she went upstairs to wash fat again. In the basement cutting room, water splashed everywhere, and blood ran freely onto the brick floor beneath her feet. She wore clumsy, wooden-soled shoes to keep her up out of the slime. One day, in the middle of the morning, she took her knife up to the fifth floor to have it sharpened. On the way down, her feet slipped and she fell down several flights of stairs. For twenty-six days, Melvina lay in bed unable to move anything but her hand. The women of the Eastern Star Club helped feed her family, and the company paid her thirty dollars for her time away from work. But when Melvina returned to the packing plant, she worked only three weeks, and then was told not to come back because she "might fall again."[47] She would not earn packing plant wages again.

As an individual, Melvina was dispensable; but as a class, black workers suddenly, because of the war, became valuable to the packing companies. In the contest between labor and employers to see which side would gain more from the pressures and opportunities of the wartime economy, the loyalty of black workers became a prize to be won.

White union leaders in 1917 knew that the government could not allow the meatpacking industry to be crippled by a strike. A powerful union and a threatened strike would, they believed, cause the government to step in and force arbitration. And any government intervention would most likely bring improved conditions and higher wages to the packing plant workers. So the leaders of several unions formed the Stockyards Labor Council and began an aggressive organizing campaign.

The packing companies, in response, determined to undercut the union organizing drive by courting the black workers and winning their loyalty. They gave financial support to black churches. They also gave money to the Urban League and collaborated with the League to place migrants in jobs. Through the South Side YMCA, packing companies sponsored glee clubs and baseball teams. All this earned the gratitude of black leaders and black workers—especially among the newly arrived, who had come north not just for jobs, but to find a place where the amenities of American life would be open to them.

While they were winning over the blacks, packing company officials threatened the white workers. In some departments, white workers reported that if "we had anything to do with the union guys, then we'd find ourselves cleaning casings while the colored girls would be on our jobs."[48]

In response to the tactics of packing company officials, the unions began to court black workers. The Stockyards Labor Council sponsored interracial picnics[49] and tried to open various unions to black membership. Here the Women's Trade Union League—just as strong in Chicago as in New York—launched its own campaign. The WTUL had been working among white women in the stockyards since a large—but failed—strike in 1904. Now that black women were coming into the yards by the thousands, they too would need the education, training, and support of the WTUL.

Irene Sappington Goines would lead the effort. Southern blacks knew very little about unions, but Goines was a northerner. Born and raised in Illinois, she had moved to Chicago in 1898, just after her marriage. She was the first director of blacks in the Illinois League of Women Voters, and when Illinois passed a law permitting woman suffrage in 1913, Goines was among the first women to

Tool room work at Winslow Brothers plant in Chicago. War Department photograph, courtesy of the National Archives at College Park (RG 165-WW-594-A-4).

register to vote. She owned and ran a millinery business, joined the Urban League, and participated in a number of women's clubs. Later in the war, she would work for the United States Employment Service and the Red Cross.[50] But in 1917 she worked primarily for the WTUL, trying to organize black women in the stockyards of Chicago.[51] It was like any other organizing work among women—passing out leaflets, holding meetings, trying to persuade the overworked and underpaid to join an organization that could get them fired. Among black women, it was especially hard. "My people" said Irene Goines, "know so little about organized labor that they have had a great fear of it."[52] They had for so long been excluded from unions, they had so often entered new trades only as strikebreakers, and now they had developed an awe for the power—and apparent benevolence—of the white packing plant owners.

Finally, a lone black woman showed up at the door during one of the white women's meetings. Chairing the meeting that night was a young woman whose father had recently quit his job when a black man had been placed beside him at work. Mary McDowell of the WTUL described the scene in the gymnasium: "Hanna, as doorkeeper, called out in her own social way, 'A colored sister is at the door. What'll I do with her?' 'Admit her,' called back the president, 'and let all of ye's give her a hearty welcome.' The tall, dignified, good-looking, well-dressed colored girl, much frightened walked down the center aisle of the gymnasium, while the room rang with cheers and the clapping of hands."[53]

The warm welcome could not, however, smooth over all of the tensions for a black minority in an essentially white union. Eventually, for both men and women, separate locals were organized for black workers in their Black Belt neighborhoods.[54] Even with their own locals, most of those who joined the stockyard unions would be settled northern blacks.

That summer, in East St. Louis, whites who had seen blacks used as strikebreakers and blacks who had always been excluded from unions clashed in a full-scale race riot. At least nine whites and many more blacks died in the streets. In Chicago, the Stockyards Labor Council struggled on with its organizing drive, and the employers continued their support of black community organizations.

Late in the fall, the Stockyards Labor Council voted to call a strike and—as predicted—the government sent in arbitrators to prevent the shutting down of the meatpacking industry. Through two months of hearings, black workers took their turn on the witness stand before Judge Samuel Alschuler, describing their lives, wages, and working conditions. The final settlement granted a large wage increase, and an eight-hour day. It allowed employers to require overtime "to assure our government an undiminished supply of meat,"[55] but required time-and-a-quarter pay for anything over forty-eight hours a week. Alschuler also ordered the packers to provide lunchrooms, washrooms, and dressing rooms in the plants. Among workers, the decision seemed a great victory. Just after the settlement, union organizers were kept busy night and day signing up new members, and they had trouble finding halls big enough for their meetings.[56] A great outdoor rally, attended by both black and white workers, celebrated the award.

Most black union members still tended to be northerners, but the campaign of 1917, and the Alschuler award, began the process of converting the southern blacks to a belief in unions. By early 1918, one Sister Stockly, a transplanted and newly converted southerner, would stand up in a union meeting to declare, "I believes in organization, redemption, and the Holy Ghost."[57] But that change would be slow to come. In the spring and summer of 1917, Irene Goines still struggled, with little success, to recruit black women. Despite all her efforts, the new migrants hung back, grateful simply to have jobs that paid cash wages.

■

In response to the American declaration of war against Germany, Austria and Turkey severed diplomatic relations with the United States.

■

Outside the stockyards, other kinds of factory work also opened up. As black men and white women moved up and out of the lowest-paying jobs, black women moved in. At glass factories, while white women were etching, sorting, and packing glass pieces, black women spent the day carrying large trays of glass back and forth over brick or concrete floors, taking glass pieces from the hot furnaces of the blowing room and putting them into the tempering ovens.[58] In commercial bakeries, they cleaned and greased the largest, heaviest pans. In waste processing factories, they replaced men at the task of sewing up bales of rags—doing work, the employer said, "that no white women would do." [59] In factories where there was no hot and heavy labor to be done, black women swept the floors and picked up refuse. For the railroads, women cleaned cars inside and out. They sorted and put away laundry for the Pullman cars, cleaned up scraps in the rail yards, moved oil barrels, and operated lift trucks for transferring freight. The young and strong even drove in spikes with sledgehammers. In Newark, New Jersey, black women found work loading shells at a munitions factory. In Philadelphia, they were employed at the big government arsenals and warehouses.

Some of these jobs were easier than working in the cotton fields and scrubbing laundry in backyard washtubs. Many of them were harder, however, than domestic service in middle-class northern households. Still, eager to escape the interminable hours of domestic work and the tensions of the servant-mistress relationship,[60] black women took industrial jobs whenever they could find them. One twenty-two-year-old, identified only as Miss T. S., had been a cook in

The Banner Manufacturing Company in Detroit. Women's Bureau photograph, courtesy of the National Archives at College Park. (RG 86G-2E-11).

Georgia. In Chicago, after finding work in a box factory, she told an investigator, "I'll never work in nobody's kitchen but my own any more."[61]

Gradually, a fortunate few began to find better jobs. With the Urban League writing letters and knocking on doors, with the club women spreading messages about how to adapt to the northern climate and northern customs and work schedules, and with more and more white women abandoning their traditional trades to take up war work, employers began to consider black women for cleaner and more skilled work. In Detroit, although most black women still worked as domestics, some began to find jobs assembling automobiles and aircraft engines.[62] The Banner Manufacturing Company, also in Detroit, was owned by African Americans and employed black women throughout the company, from machine operators to office clerks.[63] It appears to have been a model factory, well illuminated, not overcrowded, and equipped with chairs with backrests. The black community also began to provide some of its own training.

Triana Woods, a Mississippi schoolteacher, moved to Chicago in 1917 and immediately established a training school, where she taught women to operate power sewing machines.[64]

In white-owned businesses, black women began to find jobs in cigar factories, textile mills, and furniture factories. Most often, black and white women were put on separate floors or even in separate buildings—partly because some white women would not work with members of another race, and partly because separating the races allowed employers to pay black women lower wages for the same work.[65] But in these segregated shops, the African American workers began to insist on being supervised by women of their own race. At a lampshade company, when a white woman replaced the regular black supervisor, the shop became chaotic. With the return of their own forewoman, the workers were again inspired and efficient.[66]

Whenever there was an advance, or a new opportunity, readers in the North

On a segregated shop floor in New York City, women prepared "spiral puttees"—gaiters to protect the lower legs of soldiers in the field. War Department photograph, courtesy of the National Archives at College Park (RG 165-WW-585 [11]).

The note on the back of this photograph of a Pennsylvania brickyard states, "They are *girls." Women's Bureau photograph, courtesy of the National Archives at College Park (RG 86G-6S-3).*

and South learned of it in the pages of the Chicago *Defender*. "Race women" were working as truckers in a freight house in Toledo, according to one headline. In New Orleans, they were working in oil processing mills, and in that city they also began to deliver ice, driving the big horse-drawn wagons and carrying the blocks of ice into homes and restaurants. When northern-born, high school–educated black women passed the Civil Service exam and were hired as mail carriers, the *Defender* would of course announce that, too.[67]

Through the months of war and far beyond, the migration would continue, and the message that was first spread in the *Defender* would be echoed in the letters that the new migrants wrote to those who had stayed behind. They told sometimes of illness and homesickness, but also of success. "Nothing here but money and it is not hard to get," wrote one man to his old lodge brother in Alabama. The women wrote home, too. "We get $1.50 a day and we pack so many sausages we don't have much time to play," a woman wrote to her friend, "but it is a matter of a dollar with me and I feel that God made the path and I am walking therein." Still another reported with pride, "I work like a man. I am making good." [68]

CHAPTER FIVE

Mobilizing Woman Power: Washington, 1917-1918

AT TEN O'CLOCK ON AN APRIL morning in 1917, Mary Anderson got the news: "You'll have to take the noon train to Washington today," Mrs. Robins told her. Anderson was in Chicago, in the midst of organizing support for a thousand striking women, makers of small machine parts. One week into the strike, it was a very bad time for her to leave, but Margaret Dreier Robins, president of the National WTUL, insisted. Mrs. Robins herself would stay and work with "the girls" so that Anderson could go.[1]

The invitation had come — belatedly — from Samuel Gompers, president of the American Federation of Labor. Asked by Woodrow Wilson to head a labor advisory committee under the Council of National Defense, Gompers had ignored working women and formed a committee of men. And yet there were vast industries energized by the hands of women—women who were still segregated in the workplace, still underrepresented in unions, still unenfranchised in most states, but who were giving eight, ten, or twelve hours a day to the war effort. In response to Gompers's slight, the Women's Trade Union League had showered Washington with telegrams. They wrote not just to Gompers himself, but to the secretary of labor, to the secretary of war, and even to President Wilson. In response, Gompers appointed a subcommittee on Women in Industry, chaired by the wealthy Democratic Party fund-raiser and hostess Florence J. Harriman. Again he included no working women or women trade union leaders,

Mary Anderson. Photograph, courtesy of the National Archives at College Park (RG 86G-9F-3).

and again the WTUL pelted him with telegrams. Finally, Gompers appointed some trade union women, including Mary Anderson.[2] So she packed a bag and boarded the train.

She was a person who held up well under travel. Her first great journey had begun in a tiny village in Sweden, in 1889, when she was only sixteen. With her sister Hilda, Mary traveled by ship across the stormy North Atlantic to England, and then across the great ocean to Ellis Island. Then somehow, speaking no English, they made their way by train across the vast distance to Michigan, where a third sister had already settled. A sturdy, even stocky girl, Mary had loved the outdoor work on a farm. She stood five feet, six inches, tall and had a square face, brown hair, cool blue eyes, and a steady, even temperament. She learned English quickly, by speaking it, and by reading and rereading the newspaper every day. Like many immigrants, she moved from job to job, looking for better pay, more interesting work, a cleaner factory, a kinder boss. She worked as a dishwasher in a boardinghouse for lumbermen, as a maid in a private home, and then as a machine operator in garment and shoe factories in Illinois and Wisconsin.

Finally, at the age of twenty-two, Mary Anderson settled into the boot and shoe trade in Chicago, where she discovered the trade union movement. Now, instead of trying to improve her own conditions by changing jobs, she learned it was possible to improve conditions for everyone by negotiating with the employer.[3]

Full of calm common sense, she soon became a leader, first as president of the women's local of the International Boot and Shoe Workers Union, and then as their representative to the Chicago Federation of Labor. Working with the mostly male, citywide organization, she came to know the working life of the rest of the city, in the garment factories, the stockyards, the binderies, the restaurants. At the age of thirty-four she won an appointment to the executive board of the International Boot and Shoe Workers Union, and there she began to develop a national view of labor issues. She traveled to Boston twice a year for meetings, and visited shoe factories in Lynn, Massachusetts, and other strife-ridden shoe towns. The only woman on the executive board, she was also the only member not on the union payroll, and so she had to continue full-time work as a shoe stitcher.

Anderson always claimed that the long hours of work followed by long evenings of meetings and the miles of walking the Chicago streets—to and from work, to and from meetings, and among factories—were not hard physically, for the Swedish farm girl had grown into a woman of great stamina. Intellectually, she had developed into a patient and pragmatic negotiator with a strong distaste for strikes. "They involve so much suffering," she would always say. She preferred "hammering away to get a little improvement here and a change for the better there."[4] Labor organization, collective bargaining, arbitration—these were the mechanisms for creating change. The union, in her mind, was a means of avoiding strikes.

Like Rose Schneiderman in New York, Anderson discovered the Women's Trade Union League, and in 1911 she left her job as a shoe worker to become a paid organizer for the Chicago branch of the WTUL. Garment workers, stockyard workers, and hospital attendants all had the benefit, over the next six years, of having Mary Anderson on their side. For two years, the garment workers avoided strikes because seven days a week, day and night, Mary Anderson traveled through the city, educating, cajoling, interpreting, and carrying messages between the young workers, who were inclined to strike over every grievance, and the employers, who would have preferred to fire anyone who joined a union.[5] Along with Agnes Nestor—a dark-haired little glove maker—Anderson helped the nurses and attendants in Illinois hospitals win an eight-hour day, a six-day week, and a raise in pay. During the stockyard drive of January 1917, she handed out leaflets on subzero mornings.[6]

By spring of that year, the United States had entered the war and Mary Anderson had been called to Washington to serve on the Gompers committee. She was now forty-five years old, and her hair was lightly frosted with silver. She still spoke softly, with a lingering Swedish accent, but she had developed a confidence that allowed her to speak her mind and a wisdom that made others want to heed her opinions.

The Committee on Women in Industry met at the Lafayette Hotel in late April and quickly realized that they had no real power and no very clear mandate. Somehow they must help increase productivity, decrease labor strife, and protect the interests of women workers all at once. The Supreme Court, in 1908, had upheld the notion that "the mothers of the race" should be protected from hazardous chemicals, night work, and excessive hours. Now, faced with mobilizing for war, state legislatures around the country had begun to relax labor standards, especially those designed to protect women and child laborers. Mary Anderson knew from her own experience that when hours went from ten a day up to twelve or fourteen, workers actually produced fewer goods. And most everyone in Washington knew what had happened in England during the first years of the war: industrial workers had been ground down to the point of exhaustion, until finally the government established controls over industry. And so the initial task of the Committee on Women in Industry became obvious. At their very first meeting, they adopted resolutions calling on the nation to maintain labor standards, especially regarding hours of work and a day of rest. They also urged employers not to put women who had young children on night shifts, and they warned middle-class women not to undercut the wages of women who had to

Trimming currency at the Treasury Department, 1907. In early 1917, under pressure from the WTUL, the National American Woman Suffrage Association, and Jeannette Rankin—the only woman in Congress at the time—the Treasury Department shortened the hours and raised the wages of these workers. Photograph courtesy of the National Archives at College Park (121-BA-361B).

Mary Van Kleeck at her desk in Washington. Sophia Smith Collection, Smith College.

work to support themselves.[7] It was a modest and practical first statement, but it carried no particular weight.

Next the committee began collecting information on women's war work. They sent people to visit factories and armories and talk to workers and supervisors. They wrote reports and made recommendations. As Mary Anderson rode the train back and forth between Chicago and Washington to attend meetings, she began to fear that the committee would be not much more than an information exchange. With the help of Mary McDowell—also of Chicago—she put together a more specific plan of action for determining and establishing labor standards.[8] But as they struggled to find a voice, it was not at all clear who was listening.

While the committee held its meetings and issued recommendations, militant suffragists picketed the White House. A president who was waging a war to make the world safe for democracy should, they clamored, support full democracy at home. Among them, a few munitions workers from Bridgeport carried banners proclaiming the working woman's need for the ballot to protect her working conditions.[9]

Inside the Lafayette Hotel, the Committee on Women in Industry, ignoring the suffrage issue for the moment, tried to find a balance between support of war production and protection of workers. In June, a new member joined the committee—Mary Van Kleeck of the Russell Sage Foundation. Anderson described her as "a crisp, intelligent-looking person,"[10] and quickly sought her as an ally. They were not kindred spirits, but complementary minds. Anderson had lived the life of a worker and had a warm affection for working women. She knew what it was to be fired for joining a union, to be arrested on the picket line, and to be told that she didn't need to earn a living wage because she was only a girl. Van Kleeck had been only a witness to the struggle, but she had a keen intellectual understanding of the large social implications of poverty, child labor, and overwork. By the summer of 1917, at the age of thirty-five, Van Kleeck had a national reputation as a careful researcher, an able administrator, and an advocate for employment bureaus, a minimum wage, and state laws prohibiting night work for women.[11]

■

In May, Congress passed the Selective Service Act, and later that summer the first draft called up 687,000 men.[12] In mid-June, General John J. Pershing arrived in Paris to command the American Expeditionary Forces. Two weeks later, the first U.S. troops reached France.

■

On the first day they met, Mary Van Kleeck told Mary Anderson why she had come to Washington. She had been called in as a consultant to the Ordnance Department—a division within the War Department responsible for supplying the army with everything from heavy artillery to toothbrushes. As the army mobilized, all of this matériel needed to be handled, sorted, stored, and shipped, and Mary Van Kleeck was to look into the possibility of employing women in the military warehouses. The Army expected, before the end of the year, to need storage space not only for guns and ammunition, saddles and medical supplies, but for "six million pairs of shoes, ten million undershirts, thirteen million pairs of socks, and so on down the line." Wondering why the Committee on Women in Industry had not been given the task, Van Kleeck consulted her colleague from the Russell Sage Foundation, Leonard P. Ayres, who now served on the War Industries Board of the Council of National Defense. Ayres shared the general view that the women's committee was powerless and unfocused, and that "all of Mr. Gompers' work is rigidly confined to safeguarding the interests of the A.F. of L." He advised Van Kleeck to take on the project.[13]

She immediately met resistance to the very idea of putting women into warehouses. The sales manager of the Western Electric Company in Boston told her that warehouses were "the last place in the world in which to employ women." Such a rough class of men worked in warehouses, he claimed, that women could not safely mingle with them.[14] But as Van Kleeck traveled around to government storage facilities, she found that women were already inspecting and packing underwear, socks, shirts, mosquito netting, and other small articles. In her reports to Morris L. Cooke, chairman of the Storage Committee of the General Munitions Board, she pointed out that assigning women to the work required common sense: "Packing dental supplies is not the same occupation as packing saddles." In answer to the problem of safeguarding the morals and dignity of young women in warehouses, she recommended the simple solution of hiring female supervisors. To make the women comfortable, the Army could provide them with adequate rest room facilities. To help them handle heavy articles, equipment for loading and lifting could be added.[15]

During that summer, when Mary Van Kleeck was studying the question of storage work for women, the Committee on Women in Industry continued to gather information, calling upon various state committees to provide detailed studies. When New York's Committee on Women in Industry looked at factories making Army and Navy uniforms for the Brooklyn Navy Yard, they found two worlds. Much of the sewing was sent out directly to home workers, in homes that were licensed and inspected, clean and well ordered.[16] Some of the factories, too, were modern and well-lit buildings in Manhattan. Others, however, were much the same as they had always been in the worst parts of the garment trade. In Brooklyn, thousands of women worked on uniform shirts in dark and dirty factories, where the work areas were crowded and cluttered and the rest rooms were piled with broken furniture. The workers here were the young and the desperate: girls under sixteen, and Jewish, Italian, and Polish immigrants, mixed in with a few black migrants fresh from the exhausted tenant farms of the south.[17]

Altering and repairing uniforms in the tailoring shop at an army salvage plant. Photograph courtesy of the National Archives at College Park (Signal Corps photo SC111).

These shops also sent sewing out to home workers, who helped keep the hours long and the wages low for the women in the factories. Though the foremen denied sending out home work, the investigators recognized the telltale signs: children coming and going, pushing carts and baby carriages loaded with heavy wool overcoats; women negotiating with foremen and scribbling into little brown notebooks where they kept their records.[18] Because wartime inflation kept ordinary people from buying clothes, men and able young women in the regular garment factories were losing their jobs. At the same time, government work was being done in tenement kitchens—at half the wages of factory work-

The stockroom at the Watertown Arsenal. Photograph courtesy of the Schlesinger Library, Radcliffe Institute, Harvard University (PC8-2-7).

ers—by pregnant women, mothers of large families, and children.[19] The Committee on Women in Industry concluded that for the sake of the war effort, if not the welfare of the labor force, the government needed greater control and consistency in its contracts.

Meanwhile, Mary Van Kleeck continued to travel and report back to Morris Cooke at the Ordnance Department. In Norfolk, Virginia—a busy and growing port city—the Army had engaged most of the available men for construction projects in and around the shipyards. Since no men were left to work in the warehouses, Van Kleeck was to look for women. She found many women already doing industrial work in Norfolk. Three-quarters of them were blacks who were mostly working in tobacco plants, peanut processing plants, and wooden-box

Alice Dunbar-Nelson, who helped organize black women's volunteer efforts for the war, also took an interest in women's paid employment. According to Dunbar-Nelson, "'Come out of the kitchen, Mary' was the slogan of the colored woman in wartime. She doffed her cap and apron and donned her overalls." Women's Bureau photograph, courtesy of the National Archives at College Park (RG 86G-6S-7).

factories. By the fall of 1917, Van Kleeck also found African American women working in a lumberyard where they used levers to lift fifty-pound bundles of boards, and where they had begun to replace men at buzz-saw machines. White women were finding more and more jobs in offices, and they continued to monopolize the jobs in underwear knitting mills and other garment factories. But they had also begun to do some rougher work, making awnings and tents for the Army. If the warehouses needed them, many of these women—black and white—were capable of doing the work.[20]

Van Kleeck also visited the Springfield Armory in Massachusetts, where she found that women had just begun to enter the machine shops. Fifty women had been working there for only a few weeks, filing small parts and inspecting and fitting those parts. The woolen-shirt department, however, already employed about

Shacks along the riverbank in Jeffersonville, Indiana, where army shirts were made. Women's Bureau photograph, courtesy of the National Archives at College Park (RG 86G-6A-3).

two thousand women, who all worked at home, earning forty-five cents for each shirt.[21] In one of her reports to Morris Cooke, Van Kleeck warned him about the spread of disease. During the Spanish-American War, she reminded him, measles had been spread through the Army by uniforms manufactured in tenement slums.[22]

Most important, she added, the supply depot question was "but one phase of the big subject." The successful employment of women in time of war would require careful, expert study of individual workplaces. The Department of War, she concluded, should establish a women's work bureau "to study and advise" on the employment of women in all branches of work for the military.[23] At the AFL convention that fall, she showed her final storage report to Mary Anderson, who recognized the truth of the details and supported the main conclusion: the government needed a women's work bureau.

From their position on the Committee on Women in Industry, Anderson, Van Kleeck, and their colleagues could do little more than investigate and advise, but they were relentless. Amy Hewes, now executive secretary of the committee, sent a group out to look into the making of Army shirts in the little town of Jeffersonville, Indiana, which sat on the north side of the Ohio River, just opposite Louisville, Kentucky. There they found a ferryboat traveling back and forth across the river every half hour, delivering sewing work—shirts, overalls, and bed sacks—to twenty-one thousand women, both black and white, who lived and worked in shacks, barns, and shanty boats along the river. In one house, investigators found chickens and pigs mingling among the uniform shirts. In her preliminary report, Hewes noted that the women sewed with ordinary domestic sewing machines, which were slow and produced low quality work, while in the established clothing centers, workers were still being laid off.[24]

At the same time, Florence Kelley had been directly lobbying the secretary of war. Kelley had for years been a member of the National Consumers' League —a vocal organization devoted to improving working conditions through pressure from shoppers. Through that work she knew Newton Baker, a longtime member of the NCL and now Woodrow Wilson's new secretary of war. With Baker at the War Department, Kelley now had the opportunity to press directly for government action to protect garment workers. Baker had named Kelley to a three-member committee on Army clothing, and from that post she helped prepare a report on the abusive and chaotic conditions under which military uniforms were being produced. In a private letter that accompanied the formal

Loading rough lumber at Hooker Electric in Chicago. Women's Bureau photograph, courtesy of the National Archives at College Park (RG 86G-2K-2).

report, she told Secretary Baker, "There is no more time to be lost. . . . The rut of usage is deep and the Quartermasters are all in it. You alone can get them out. We outsiders are valueless in their eyes. To them we are civilians, theorists without experience." The current specifications, she added "are a disgrace to the Quartermasters, because they omit all safeguards for labor conditions."[25]

Baker took the problem seriously enough to delegate it to Felix Frankfurter. A dapper little man with a round face, a passion for efficiency, and an ambition that would eventually lead him to the Supreme Court, Frankfurter had left his professorship at Harvard Law School to take a post in the office of the secretary of war. He had been a soapbox orator himself, before becoming an attorney; he had been enthralled by Rose Schneiderman's speeches; and in January of 1917, he had worked with the National Consumers' League on defending minimum wage and maximum hours legislation.[26] He agreed with Florence Kelley that without some sort of order imposed by Washington, the garment industry—under pressure of war orders—would begin to devour its own workers. Brilliant and charismatic, Frankfurter had the personal power to cut through red tape. By the end of the summer, he had drafted a standard contract for all factories producing uniforms and had begun to increase the number of government inspectors who would enforce the new code.[27] Gradually, the assembly and finishing of Army uniforms would be pushed out of the tenement homes and back into the factories.

Turmoil in the garment industry was not, of course, the only problem. At a November meeting of the Committee on Women in Industry, Mary McDowell reported on unhealthy conditions at the freight yards in Chicago, Cleveland, and Rochester. In December, the committee heard a report on the Frankford Arsenal, just outside of Philadelphia, where the health and safety standards recommended by the chief of ordnance were routinely ignored. During the committee's lunch break that day, Mary Van Kleeck drafted a resolution reaffirming the group's "conviction that the labor laws must be maintained and enforced," and the committee signed it in the afternoon.[28] Still, Mary Anderson was restless. She was accustomed to having a seat at the negotiating table; this committee was little more than a nag and a nuisance.

■

In the fall of 1917, the Allies suffered a series of military disasters in Europe. In October, Austria-Hungary broke through the Italian lines at Caporetto, and in November the British and Canadian armies suffered defeat at the Third Battle of Ypres, losing 400,000 men and leaving their armies close to exhaustion. In Russia, the Provisional Government was overthrown by the Bolsheviks.

■

Back in Chicago, through the WTUL, Mary Anderson could work more directly to improve conditions and wages. The stockyards organizing campaign had continued through the summer and into the fall, and Anderson had joined Irene Goines in passing out leaflets and holding meetings, trying to persuade the women, including newly arrived black women, to join the unions.

Similar efforts were under way in industries around the country as workers responded to the frenzied wartime economy. Wages of skilled laborers—machinists, iron molders, carpenters—kept going up, but the paychecks of the great masses of low-skill workers could barely keep up with inflation. While they struggled to pay their bills and to buy war bonds, and while they sent their young men off to fight in Europe, American workers watched munitions companies gather large war profits. In protest, American workers staged more than four thousand strikes during that first year at war—more strikes than ever before in any one year.[29] In the West, mining and lumber industries became chaotic; across the country strikes and lockouts created bottlenecks. Social order, too, began to succumb to the pressures over job turmoil, inflated prices, and the housing shortage in industrial centers. In early July, these tensions exploded in a bloody race riot in East St. Louis. By late fall, competition and mismanagement on the railroads had begun to strangle the nation's transportation system.

Faced with increasing turmoil, government leaders had to act. In December, the presidential mediation commission went to Chicago to settle the packing industry strike. At the same time, President Wilson seized the railroads and put them under federal administration for the duration of the war. By early 1918, he would establish a War Labor Board to mediate—and if necessary impose—solutions in industrial disputes.

■

On January 8, before a joint session of Congress, Woodrow Wilson presented America's war aims through his soon-to-be-famous "Fourteen Points." He called for open covenants of peace, freedom of the seas, removal of economic barriers, reduction of arms, a general association of nations, German evacuation of occupied territories, and self-determination of the peoples of Eastern Europe. Still hoping for a "peace without victory," he called for no reparations or punishment for the defeated nations.

■

Amid all this pressure to establish some sort of coherence in America's labor policy, the Ordnance Department finally took Mary Van Kleeck's advice. It was time to get some key women out of the advisory committees and place them more directly into the government. Van Kleeck's experience as an administrator at the Russell Sage Foundation, combined with her proven value as a researcher, made her an obvious choice to head the new women's division. In January, she became director of the Woman's Branch of the Industrial Service Section of the Ordnance Department, U.S. Army. Accepting the job, Van Kleeck said that she wanted a true labor woman with her, someone with both experience and credibility. She chose Mary Anderson to be her assistant director.[30]

The use of pulleys lightened the work at the Pierce-Arrow Motor Corporation factory. By the end of the war, more than one in ten auto workers were female. Women's Bureau photograph, courtesy of the National Archives at College Park (RG 86G-1P-1).

Their task would be "to free the best energies of women workers" by enforcing labor standards in the government arsenals and in factories working under military contracts. Anderson took a three-month leave of absence from the Women's Trade Union League and joined Van Kleeck at offices in the Army and Navy building in Washington.[31] They were the first women to do anything more than clerical or janitorial work in the War Department.

Mary Van Kleeck had already helped write General Orders 13, issued by General William Crozier, chief of ordnance. Not truly orders, but rather a recommended set of standards, the document stressed the need for reasonable working hours, healthy working conditions, equal pay for equal work, and the right to organize. Now it was time to put the document to work. The new Women's Branch immediately dispatched representatives around the country to monitor military work. Amy Hewes was sent repeatedly to the upper Midwest to oversee sixty-eight plants doing government work. Other representatives went to Philadelphia and Boston.[32] Van Kleeck and Anderson put a female personnel director in every government arsenal and helped establish a course at Mt. Holyoke College, taught by Amy Hewes, for training health officers to serve in factories.[33] They understood that change would not be instantaneous, but now they could help increase production at the same time that they safeguarded the health of workers.

They were probably not surprised when they met with resistance. Men at similar levels in the government had been put into uniform and handed commissions that gave them instant authority. When the women of the Ordnance Department showed up at a factory that had government contracts, they had difficulty even getting through the door. And when they did get in, they were so closely escorted and controlled that they often learned very little. Anderson began to think that, at the end of her three months, she would return to her work with the Women's Trade Union League in Chicago.[34] But official Washington was not to let her go.

While the Ordnance Department had been reorganizing, there were changes under way at the Department of Labor as well. The indefatigable Felix Frankfurter was now working with Secretary of Labor William B. Wilson, looking for ways to give the government more control over labor policy. To study the problem, they first established an advisory council made up of two representatives of labor, two of employers, and three of the public, including one woman—Agnes Nestor. The former glove maker, who had worked with Mary Anderson on labor issues in Chicago, was now president of the Chicago Women's Trade Union League. Nestor was a tiny woman with a sweet, girlish face, a shrewd mind, and an enormous handbag full of reports and legal briefs. In 1909 she had helped win passage of a ten-hour day law for working women in Illinois, and when that bill had finally passed, she had immediately begun a campaign for an eight-hour law. She had been called to Washington in 1914, serving first on the national Vocational Education Commission and then on Anna Howard Shaw's Woman's Committee, which was overseeing all of women's war efforts, from food conservation to volunteer ambulance driving. Now, in the early months of 1918, Agnes Nestor had been selected to represent all of American womanhood in the task of setting up a labor department that would help win the war. Mary Anderson wrote from Chicago advising her to ask for a decent salary and a secretary.[35]

The Women's Trade Union League had been arguing for years in favor of a women's division within the Department of Labor. Now, with the nation at war and with the persistent and persuasive Agnes Nestor on the advisory council, the women's division was sure to happen. In late January, Mary Anderson heard from Nestor that the council was meeting every day. Under the new plan, Nestor said, the Gompers committee activities would be taken over by the Department of Labor. "I understand the Council of Defense offices are dead these days, nothing to do. . . . [O]ld committees here seem to be just waiting for developments."[36]

Letters and telegrams darted around from Chicago to New York to Washington, as the WTUL tried to influence selection of the head of the proposed women's division. Jane Addams telegraphed the names of Mary Van Kleeck and Grace and Edith Abbott. Mary Anderson and Olive Sullivan wanted the job to go to Mary Dreier of New York, and Margaret Dreier Robins sent a list that included Mary Anderson. Rose Schneiderman worried that the League women always put forward the same few names, but probably knew that she herself could not get any sort of government appointment because of her socialist and antiwar views.[37] In the end, the choice may have been made by Felix Frankfurter.

■

On March 3, the new Bolshevik government of Russia signed a peace treaty with Germany, leaving the Central Powers free to focus on the Western Front. As the Germans gathered strength in France, Allied leaders intensified their calls for American troops, warning that the war would be lost unless they arrived quickly.

■

Frankfurter was living at the time in a house on Nineteenth Street, along with a collection of other single young men of a progressive bent. The House of Truth, as it was called, attracted some of the brightest thinkers, writers, artists, and politicians of the day for dinner and debate.[38] Shortly after the Advisory Commission submitted its report, Frankfurter invited Mary Anderson to have lunch at the House of Truth along with six or seven men. It was an uncomfortable and embarrassing ordeal, as they were clearly evaluating her.[39] But her calm self-assurance must have impressed them, and her decisive actions with Mary Van Kleeck at the Ordnance Department had apparently earned the two women a reputation as an effective team.

Van Kleeck was out of town on an inspection tour, and so it was Mary Anderson who was summoned the next day to see Secretary Wilson. "I want to move you and Miss Van Kleeck over here to take charge of the Woman in Industry Service," he told her. "I don't know which of you ought to be the director and which the assistant, but you can settle that between you." Anderson replied that Mary Van Kleeck had greater administrative experience and so should be director. She then wired Van Kleeck, telling her to come back to Washington immediately. After a brief conference, they went to see Wilson to say that they would take on the job.[40] And so Mary Van Kleeck became director of the new Woman in Industry Service, with Mary Anderson as assistant director, though Van Kleeck insisted that they were in truth codirectors.[41]

Congress authorized a budget of forty thousand dollars for the Woman in Industry Service, and the two Marys, along with two secretaries, set up shop in a one-room office at the Labor Department. With a couple of wooden desks, a typewriter, and a telephone they were to oversee the working conditions of ten million working women.

Almost immediately, they came into conflict with Felix Frankfurter, who should have been their natural ally. In the reorganization of the Labor Department, he had been appointed chair of the powerful War Labor Policies Board, which was to establish standards for industries working on war contracts. Along with most of the other men in town, Frankfurter expected Anderson and Van Kleeck to develop a list of industries that could safely employ women. On a warm day in early summer, they walked with him to a park near the Washington Monument and the two women in their tidy skirts sat on a bench, while Frankfurter lounged on the grass at their feet. Van Kleeck and Anderson argued

In the gluing room at the Bohn Refrigerator Company. Women's Bureau photograph, courtesy of the National Archives at College Park (RG 86G-7D-1).

that a list of acceptable industries was both impossible and impractical. Women could work in almost any industry if the conditions were managed right.

As they talked, all three became agitated. Frankfurter wanted a simple solution and hinted that he could, if he chose, turn the matter over to some other agency. Van Kleeck and Anderson explained it again. As Mary Van Kleeck had written in her storage report, "packing dental supplies is not the same job as packing saddles." Why would one want a blanket policy that would keep women out of warehouses, if they could contribute to the war effort by packing dental supplies and other light objects? Instead of a list of "safe" industries, the Woman in Industry Service could develop a set of standards for working conditions, similar to those in General Orders 13. Any factory that could meet these standards could safely employ women. In this scheme, women would be far more available for war work, and yet their health and safety would be protected. Finally, they brought Frankfurter around.[42] Their agency would not be asked to develop a list that would exclude women from certain industries.

And so the work of the Woman in Industry Service began in the summer of 1918, just when the suffrage pickets stationed outside the White House began to be attacked by onlookers, who accused them of being unpatriotic, and to be arrested by the police, who claimed they created a disturbance. But around the city, women who still could not vote in national elections were gradually coming to have a direct voice in the running of the government.

In office buildings, converted houses, and hotel banquet rooms, as the government lurched toward a rational management of the war, the role of women grew. The National War Labor Board, which had been assigned the task of mediating industrial disputes, placed two women on its staff to advise women work-

Fumigating cotton and working with other hazardous materials, women helped bring new safety measures into industry. Women's Bureau photograph, courtesy of the National Archives at College Park (RG 86G-11A-22).

ers during the negotiations and hearings. At the Ordnance Department, Clara Tead replaced Van Kleeck and Anderson. At the same time, more women were working at lower levels. In the War Department, the Labor Department, the Treasury Department, and the Census Bureau, thousands of women found jobs as filing clerks, stenographers, typists, and bookkeepers. When Van Kleeck and Anderson pointed out that 60 percent of Civil Service exams were open only to men, the remaining exams were opened to women within two weeks.[43] Black women, too, began to find clerical jobs, though they had separate offices, separate toilets, and separate lunchrooms.[44]

At best, Washington in summer is hot; at worst, it is a steamy subtropical swamp. In their office at the Department of Labor, electric fans blew papers around as Mary Anderson and Mary Van Kleeck worked through the day and late into the evening almost every day, perfecting the language of their standards and collecting data to support their most important positions. If they were not in the office, it was because they were on the road. Crisscrossing the country, they slept in Pullman cars at night and spent their days visiting factories, talking to local officials, and making recommendations to employers.[45]

Later, Mary Anderson would suggest adding a black woman to the staff. In her work in Chicago during the stockyards organizing campaign, she had come to appreciate the peculiar needs of working African American women, and especially the difficulty of winning for them the same standards that were being insisted upon for white women. And so Helen Brooks Irvin, a teacher at the Miner Normal School in Washington and an active volunteer in wartime Washington society, joined the staff at the Labor Department, along with an African American secretary. Like Anderson and Van Kleeck, Mrs. Irvin visited factories, met with local welfare agencies, and agitated for better working conditions, not only in the arsenals and war factories, but in the laundries, on the railroads, and in the hotels and restaurants where 3 million black women were employed.[46]

■

That summer, the Germans were heading toward Paris in a great rush, hoping to get there before the Americans arrived in full force. By the first of June, they were forty-six miles from Paris. At Château-Thierry and the battle of Belleau Wood, the newly arrived American forces defeated the seasoned German troops, but lost more than ten thousand men.

■

In this second summer of war, the need for women workers continued to grow. Every day thousands of men boarded troop transport ships,[47] and the Army had plans to draft 2 or 3 million more men. To outfit that force, procurement officers warned that they would need millions of shoes, coats, gloves, and undergarments, along with more than fifteen thousand guns and millions of tons of ammunition.[48] Pressure was coming from the Allies to produce aircraft and ships in numbers beyond anything that had been contemplated in the United States. The National Industrial Conference Board pointed out that the need for women in industry could only go up. If American women were to take on war work in the same proportion as British women, 8 million more American women would be needed.[49]

In New York, as in other states, the legislature tried to repeal maximum hours laws for women in war industries. Rose Schneiderman testified against the bill only to be called an "unpatriotic parasite" and to be labeled "Red Rose" for her socialist leanings. Although the head of the War Labor Board in Washington supported a maximum eight-hour day, the New York bill repealing maximum hours passed both houses. It was finally vetoed by the governor,[50] but the conflict over the sustaining power of workers, which had concerned Mary Van Kleeck from the beginning of her career, would continue throughout the war.

Working in collaboration with Clara Tead at Ordnance, Van Kleeck and Anderson were able to get their new work standards inserted into military contracts: an eight-hour day and a forty-eight-hour week, established lunch and rest periods, no night work except with special permission, equal pay for women doing the same work as men, a safe and sanitary working environment, protection from hazardous chemicals, no industrial home work, a wage high enough to support dependents, worker involvement in creating good working conditions, and the establishment of personnel departments.[51]

Before the war, the government had not dared to intrude so directly into employment conditions, and most Americans had not thought such intrusion necessary. Protective laws had been passed only with great difficulty, and they remained highly controversial. As long as most working women could wear ankle-length skirts on the job, as long as they were occupied in the traditional feminine tasks of spinning, sewing, cleaning, and food preparation—however industrialized those tasks had become—many Americans could continue to imagine that traditional concepts of feminine delicacy were not being violated. When war work required women to wear bloomers and to get machine oil—

The Woman in Industry Service found that more than thirty-seven thousand women took men's places in metal-working jobs. Women were found to be especially quick with drill press work. Women's Bureau photograph, courtesy of the National Archives at College Park (RG 86G-1P-3).

rather than food products—under their fingernails, when they were packing explosives rather than candies and inspecting bullets for eight hours a day rather than inspecting corsets for twelve, when the quality of their work could directly influence the outcome of the war, their hours and wages and working conditions suddenly became the business of the public and the government.

The standards would apply first to women in industry, because most women, according to the Woman in Industry Service, went home after a day of factory work to do several hours of heavy housework.[52] Then gradually, subversively, Mary Anderson and Mary Van Kleeck began to articulate a new philosophy: it was not the person who should be regulated, but the job.

■

All of Europe's armies had suffered tremendous casualties, but American troops were now arriving at the rate of three hundred thousand a month.[53] On the Western Front in mid-July, French, British, American, and Belgian troops began to beat back the Germans. To the southeast, the Austrians had been left to face the Italians alone but planned, nevertheless, an advance across the Piave River. Austrian deserters—driven by hunger—alerted the Italian commanders to the coming attack. In early July, the Italians pushed the Austrians back across the Piave.[54]

■

In late July, the Manufacturers' Association of Niagara Falls wrote to the Department of Labor asking permission to put women on night work. They understood the special hazards—social isolation, exhaustion brought on by caring for the home and children all day and then working all night. Still, they believed that the war emergency justified an exemption from the New York State law forbidding night work for women, and they suggested that hiring sturdy Polish and Italian peasants somehow made the request tolerable: "The only remedy is to surplant this man shortage with women of those European States accustomed to laboring work," the association argued, "and repulsive as this may appear to Americans, it is a war necessity and as easily stopped upon war ending as it is to introduce it."[55]

To Van Kleeck, the issue of night work was secondary. She knew that in 1912, in the wake of the Triangle Shirtwaist fire, the New York State Factory Investigating Commission had found dangerous and unhealthy working conditions in the chemical industries of Niagara Falls,[56] which produced picric acid for

The United War Work campaign encouraged Americans to support organizations that provided services to war workers. Poster by Ernest Hamlin Baker, courtesy of Archives and Special Collections, University of Nebraska–Lincoln Libraries.

At the United Gas Improvement plant in Philadelphia, coal was transformed into manufactured gas, used primarily for lighting. Women's Bureau photograph, courtesy of the National Archives at College Park (RG 86G-6S-4).

explosives, abrasive products for heavy machinery, storage batteries, electrodes, and a great variety of caustic and poisonous chemicals.[57] In wartime, all of these products were in ever greater demand.

Van Kleeck immediately formed a committee of experts to study the employment of women in hazardous industries, and announced that their first investigation would be at Niagara Falls. Even more quickly, she sent Mary Anderson on a midnight train to Niagara Falls to have a look around. There Anderson found workers' houses sitting in the shadows of trees that had been stripped bare of their leaves by the chemicals floating out of the nearby factories. Inside the plants, women were not directly handling lead, which was known to cause miscarriages and birth defects, but they were working near processes that involved lead. In other shops, women were making Carborundum grinding wheels, working in rooms where the metallic dust was "so thick you could hardly see the worker at the next machine."[58]

Anderson's brief visit reinforced the need for urgent action. In August, Mary Van Kleeck went to Niagara Falls herself, along with four physicians, an officer from the Ordnance Department, and Nelle Swartz of the New York Department of Labor.[59] They visited the plants, interviewed welfare workers, spoke with pastors of the Polish and Italian communities, and questioned the employers about their plans and needs. They quickly concluded that the labor shortage in Niagara Falls had been a problem long before the war began taking young men away. Unhealthy working conditions, miserable housing, and frequent illness had long made it impossible for the local industries to keep workers on the job. In one of the most spectacular resorts in America, it was said that the workforce changed as quickly as the tourist population.[60]

Van Kleeck knew from the outset that she would use the Niagara Falls inves-

As a woman machines carbon at the Hooker Electric-Chemical Company in Niagara Falls, a flimsily attached exhaust hood carries away debris. Women's Bureau photograph, courtesy of the National Archives at College Park (RG 86G-2K-1).

tigation to do more than make, or reinforce, policies on night work. "The whole purpose of the investigation," she would later write, "was to secure prompt action to improve conditions in the plants."[61] Chemical industries must install blowers and filters to clean the air. They must put down impermeable flooring to replace wooden surfaces that held the poisons. They should supply bubbling drinking fountains rather than pails of water, provide plentiful soap and water for washing, and set up eating areas away from work areas. They must hire physicians to test for industrial disease, and they must rotate workers through the most hazardous tasks.

From their position at the Woman in Industry Service, Anderson and Van Kleeck could not regulate conditions for men, but they could insist that conditions be improved before women were hired. They could refuse to let women work at night if a factory might, by improving conditions, make everyone more efficient and so make night work unnecessary. And they could urge, repeatedly, that "risks should be eliminated for men" as well.[62] "The great task now," Van Kleeck wrote, "is not to set apart women from industry, but to apply the medical and engineering knowledge of the country to making all work safe and healthful for the men and women who are producing for the Nation's needs."[63]

In late September, while Van Kleeck and Anderson were studying the issue of night work and women's exposure to hazardous chemicals, the national woman suffrage amendment again came before the Congress. President Wilson had first supported it back in January, when it passed in the House but was defeated in the Senate. This time, Wilson appeared before the Senate to make a strong appeal: "We have made partners of the women in this war; shall we admit them only to a partnership of suffering and sacrifice and toil and not to a partnership of privilege and right?" He cited women's efforts in industry "wherever men have worked," as well as in Europe "upon the very skirts and edges of the battle itself," where women were serving as nurses in the Red Cross, hostesses in canteens, drivers, and telephone operators. Approval of woman suffrage, Wilson urged, was "vital to the winning of the war and to the energies alike of preparation and of battle."[64]

The Senate defeated woman suffrage again; but women toiled on, in the factories, shipyards, and machine shops, on the railroads, and in government offices. With each passing week, women were moving into jobs where they had never been before.

CHAPTER SIX

On the Shop Floor: 1918

HUTCHINSON—"HUTCH" they called her—liked to roll up her sleeves and flex her biceps, in the pose of prizefighters on the sports pages. She was a shell turner on the night shift in one of the great munitions factories near Chicago, and she delighted in her newly discovered competence in a man's job. As she worked through the night, her overalls and forearms became splattered with oil. She wore a workman's cap with a long, black visor to cut down the glare from the electric lights. As each huge shell came under her hand, delivered by a man, she grasped it in the jaws of a crane that hoisted it up into position on her lathe. Wrestling the shell into place, she fixed it in the grip of the machine, then shifted a gear to make the lathe spin. Next she set in motion the cutting tool that slowly moved along the spinning shell, cleaning and shaping it. As the cutting tool trimmed off long spirals of thin steel, she measured the shell with large calipers, until shape and size were perfect.

Hutch had been raised by her older sister. The sister's husband had died and her son had gone off to fight the war; so it was up to Hutch to support the family. She gave up an office job to become a shell turner, and began earning more than fifty dollars each week. Low-skilled workers in the same plant—women who merely sharpened tools or trucked them from one department to another—earned no more than twenty dollars a week. But Hutch had acquired a valuable skill. As the inspector slipped his gauge over her finished shells, she smiled with pride. "Oh, I guess I can manage till the boy gets back."[1]

The passage into machine shops and arsenals was not always easy for Hutch and women like her. During the early part of the war, women had moved en

A tool sharpener at the Newark shipyard. Women's Bureau photograph, courtesy of the National Archives at College Park (RG 86G-7A-15).

masse from the needle trades, sales, and food preparation into female ghettos within the munitions factories. Gradually, as more and more men were drafted into the Army, women like Hutch had to be trained for skilled machine work, and they had to be put to work alongside men. Often their former jobs and their formal education had done little to prepare them. And while the women were not in all ways ready for the shops, neither were the shops quite ready for the women.

Inside the Arsenals: Philadelphia, Pennsylvania, and Rock Island, Illinois

The nation had come to understand that it truly was at war. Newspapers printed long columns of the names of men killed in combat, and on Sundays, in the photo section, they ran pictures of muddy trenches and ruined villages in France and Italy. Semiofficial slacker raids rounded up young men and detained any who could not produce a draft registration card. The army's provost marshal issued a "work or fight" order that moved unemployed men to the top of the draft lists, while state and city laws began to require all able-bodied people to be gainfully employed. Though such laws were not applied to white women they were used to force black women, and men of all races, to stay in their jobs.[2] Quitting, or going on strike, suddenly, if indirectly, became dangerous. Labor agitators with the IWW were being imprisoned or deported. Meanwhile, propaganda posters demonized the enemy—"the bloody Hun." Food conservation drives and war bond drives put pressure on family finances and family life.

With America fully at war, the atmosphere in the arsenals was intense, and the pressures of war now included the unaccustomed mingling of men and women on the job. Men disliked having their domain invaded by women. They didn't know how to treat women in the workplace, and they didn't want to learn. More important, they feared for their jobs and their wages. The work of skilled craftsmen was being broken down into simpler tasks that could be repeated over and over by the low-skilled newcomers. And the women were turning out to be speed demons. Paper-box makers, glove workers, button makers, women who had spent years sewing the same seam in thousands of corsets a week—they all worked as if there might be no tomorrow. For in the seasonal women's trades there often was no work tomorrow. Skilled craftsmen, on the other hand, frequently worked in well-organized union shops where the men deliberately set a moderate pace, maintaining a sense of dignity and a measure of

A lathe operator at the General Electric plant in Fort Wayne, Indiana. Women's Bureau photograph, courtesy of the National Archives at College Park (RG 86G-2J-12).

resistance to the managers' attempts at control. The conflict between these two work ethics, and the belief that "men's work" might become "women's work," created a kind of gender war in some shops.[3]

At the Philadelphia Navy Yard, men shouted insults and obscenities at women entering the yard for the night shift and again leaving in the early morning hours, until the police and Navy Yard orderlies began to escort the women home.[4] At the Schuylkill Arsenal in South Philadelphia, men went into the toilet rooms and deliberately left the doors open, in order to embarrass the women, until Mary Anderson recommended installing swinging doors.[5] In other factories, men stripped off their own clothes right at their machines, and they tried to watch the women change into their overalls.[6] In many places, men simply refused to work alongside women.

When Mary Van Kleeck sent out her representatives from the Ordnance Department and then from the Woman in Industry Service, they dealt with these issues of harassment as well as questions of safety, hours, and fair wages. She assigned Helen Bryan to the Rock Island Arsenal in Illinois, where the first women had arrived on the shop floor at the end of May 1918. The women operated drill presses, punch presses, and milling machines; they assembled rifles; they sorted and sewed leather parts in the harness shop; they assembled fuses and detonators; they directly replaced men in the blueprint room and drafting room, and even in the chemical laboratories. Eventually there were more than one thousand women at the arsenal. But there were twelve thousand men, and so the presence of women continued to seem like an anomaly.

The Watertown Arsenal. Photograph courtesy of the Schlesinger Library, Radcliffe Institute, Harvard University (PC-8-2-11).

Pressing out channel iron at the Detroit Steel Products Company. According to a prewar study, 80 percent of accidents in the metal trades occurred on punch presses, which cut off fingers and mangled hands of workers. Women's Bureau photograph, courtesy of the National Archives at College Park (RG 86G-7A-32).

Under pressure from the Ordnance Department, working conditions at Rock Island were set up not to integrate but to separate the women. They started work a half hour later and went home fifteen minutes earlier than the men, so that they could travel to and from work without being harassed in the yard and jostled on the overcrowded streetcars. They ate in their own lunchroom, newly built to accommodate them. In the freshly installed locker rooms, women changed from their georgette blouses, shawls, and velvet hats into womanalls if they worked with heavy machines and chemicals, or black skirts and tailored blouses if they worked in the harness shop. A matron had charge of the rest rooms and kept a first-aid jar for treating minor injuries: small chemical burns, a finger bruised under a punch press, a thumb run through with a needle.

After the women came, the men were also given new locker rooms, better dressing and toilet rooms, and a new lunchroom. Still, the men would not allow the women to join their unions and tried to keep women from being trained for skilled machining jobs. Within the molders' union, a member could be fined for teaching any part of the trade to a woman.[7]

If white women suffered discrimination, black women suffered from it twice as much. At the Frankford Arsenal, Jeanie Hughs of the Ordnance Department carefully interviewed African American women, selecting intelligent workers to hire as inspectors, only to have them, in the end, all assigned to outdoor work.[8]

Rivet heaters and passers at the Puget Sound Navy Yard. Women's Bureau photograph, courtesy of the National Archives at College Park (RG 86G-11F-7).

In some of the shipyards, however, the feverish pace of mobilization allowed men and women, black and white, to work together. At the beginning of the war, American ships carried only a very small part of the country's overseas trade. By mid-1918, the Emergency Fleet Corporation had built American shipping into a dynamo that produced as many ships in six months as the entire industrial world normally produced in a year.[9] In this frantic buildup, women took their places on rivet gangs, heating the rivets at a forge and tossing them to the men who hammered rivets into place. In one plant, a woman heating rivets for two gangs of men wanted to quit because her wages were too low. The men, knowing that their own efficiency would drop if she left, chipped in to raise her pay to two dollars per day.[10] Other women were trained to work indoors, first as tool sharpeners and later as skilled machinists producing steel parts for the ships that would transport troops, airplanes, guns, and ammunition across the ocean.

■

On the morning of August 8, British and French troops attacked the German lines northeast of Paris. Under pounding artillery barrages and the sudden advance of 456 tanks, the demoralized German soldiers collapsed and threw down their weapons. The Allies took twenty-one thousand prisoners in four days. General Ludendorff would call this "the black day of the German army."[11]

■

The Vestibule School: Dayton, Ohio

"Few women know anything about fractions of the inch below quarters and many do not know even this," or so believed J. V. Hunter, the man in charge of training women for work at the Gisholt Machine Company.[12] Other managers had similar views. Peter O'Shea, writing for *Industrial Management,* claimed that "machine work is not like sewing—good enough or not according to the feelings of the seamstress." Machine work must be measured by rigid tests, held to strict tolerances.[13] How, then, to train uninitiated women for the precision work of a machine shop? It seemed like a puzzle at first, but the industrial managers took on the job with great relish.

In the pages of *Industrial Management,* C. U. Carpenter of the Recording and Computing Machines Company, in Dayton, wrote about "How We Trained 5000 Women" to do precision machine work. While factories that had previously

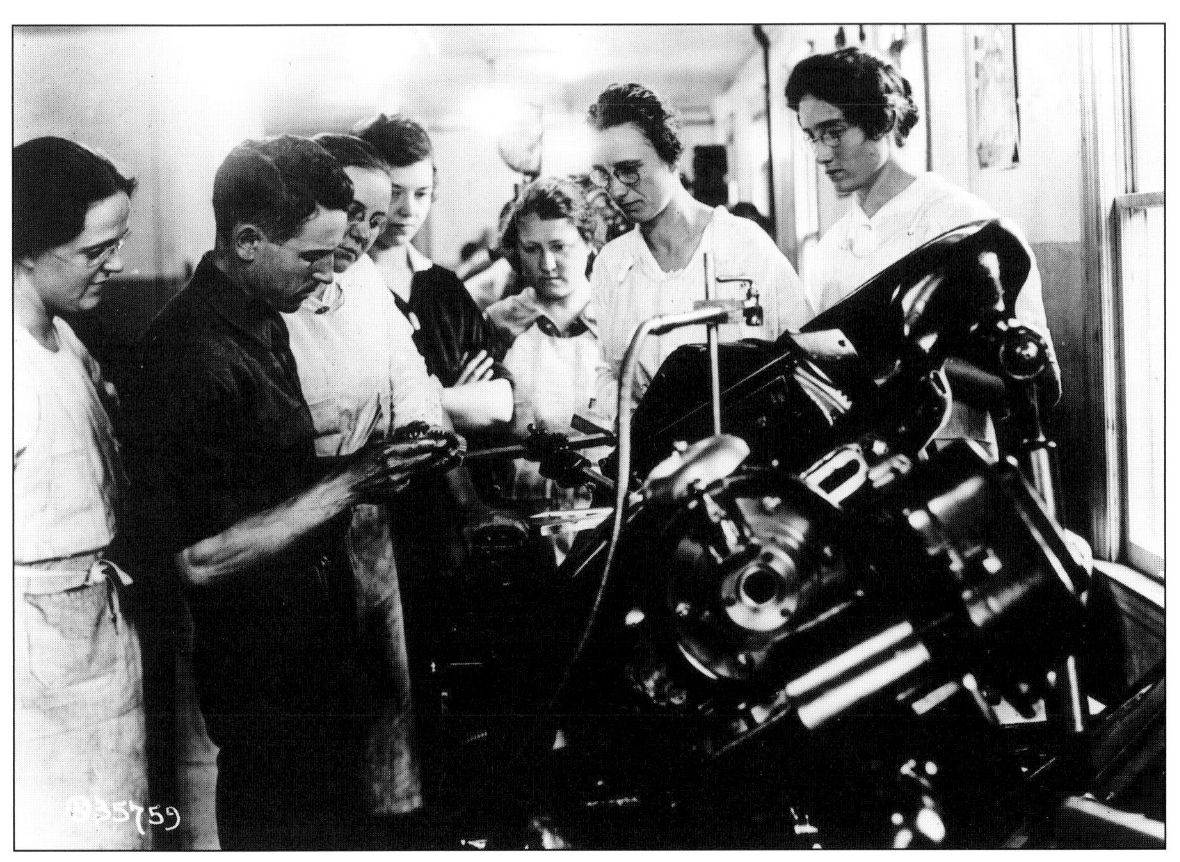

The training school at Lincoln Motors, where women helped make the huge, twelve-cylinder Liberty engines. Photograph courtesy of the Library of Congress (Signal Corps photo LC-US-Z62-111144 [229893]).

made safes and radiators were recruited to make bombs and heavy artillery,[14] the Recording and Computing Machine Company had been set to work building time fuses. The factory needed workers who could machine aluminum, brass, and other metals to within tolerances as tight as 0.0005 inch, and who could then assemble and inspect the delicately wrought devices.

When the first women were hired, Carpenter noticed that they were "very nervous—badly frightened." Some of them would "break down and weep because of the actual fear that took hold of them when they first stood before a big machine tool, the like of which they had never seen before, the uses of which they could not conceive."[15] The more earnest the girl, according to Carpenter, the more terrified she would be; and so the foremen lost patience and fired the very women who might have turned out to be the best workers.

Faced with these nervous women, the company quickly realized that what it needed was a training school: a separate space, clean and well lighted, overseen by a man selected not only for his technical skill but for his ability to behave as a gentleman. Often these schools were just inside the factory doors—near the daylight and sounds of the world outside the factory—and so they came to be known as vestibule schools. At the Recording and Computing Company, although the school was headed by a man, the actual teachers were all women. Carpenter

In shops without training schools, women got their instruction from skilled mechanics right on the shop floor. This photograph, from the Newark shipyard, shows a woman being taught to use a power chisel. Women's Bureau photograph, courtesy of the National Archives at College Park (RG 86G-7A-31).

had the idea that when a new employee came into the training department, the very first thing she should see was another woman successfully operating the strange machines. In this carefully structured atmosphere, the women were taught the function of each tool and the use of the measuring gauges. No attempt was made in this school to turn the women into all-around machinists; there was simply no time. Each was trained to become skilled in one job, operating one machine. In ten days or less, the women were sent out onto the shop floor where, according to Carpenter, "they attack[ed] their machines with vigor and confidence." In three more weeks, they were producing enough to earn bonuses for themselves and their foremen.

In the departments where workers first went through the training school, production went up beyond what any of the efficiency experts had predicted.[16] "Dilution" of skill had turned out to be not just a necessity of war, but a creator of efficiency. Instead of a roomful of all-around machinists, each one setting and resetting his machine as he changed from one operation to another, a company could put one machinist in a room with a group of moderately trained women. Each woman had to perform only one task, or operate only one machine. When the machine needed to be reset for a new task, or repaired, a highly skilled man was at hand.

Carpenter took special delight in his company's transformation of the relationship between the foremen and the women workers. By removing from the foreman the ability to hire and fire—and instead putting these tasks under control of a personnel department—the company released workers from many of the petty tyrannies of shop foremen. By tying the foreman's pay to the output of his department, the company inspired him to help and encourage new workers. The bonus system was carefully designed to make even the less expert workers strive for high output and take pride in good work. Patriotism alone could not inspire top performance and full cooperation day after day, month after month. New management strategies, according to Carpenter, could keep the "working body filled with enthusiasm and willing to respond to any call for extra effort."[17]

■

In the Balkans, Allied troops under a French commander attacked and overran Bulgarian forces. British aircraft pounded the retreating troops with bombs, creating panic within the army and among the citizens.

■

Jones and Lamson: Springfield, Vermont

It's not likely that the first women at the Jones and Lamson Machine Company wept in the presence of great machines or suffered significant harassment from the men in the shops. They lived in a machine tool town, and they were the daughters, sisters, wives, and sweethearts of skilled machinists, the cream of the industrial working class.[18] When war work called, they moved smoothly into their new roles.

Sixty years earlier, a handful of Yankee geniuses had created the American machine tool industry in the Upper Connecticut River Valley, and their successors had managed to grow the industry without growing a city. Here, in the small

The Jones and Lamson company in Springfield, Vermont. Photograph courtesy of the Springfield Art and Historical Society (1165).

towns of Springfield and Windsor, were made the machines that made interchangeable parts. In wartime, "Precision Valley" made the machines that made weapons and ammunition.

America had already been at war for many months before the Springfield industries began to hire women. At first, the labor pool was filled out by men coming in from the local farms, and by skilled factory men moving in from other places. By the first autumn of the war, the town of six thousand was "swarming like an anthill," according to a local news article, and housing became a problem, as it was in any town with significant war industries.[19] Then in December of 1917, Jones and Lamson received an order from the Watertown Arsenal to build, in addition to machine tools, the recoil mechanism for 240-mm howitzers.[20] With war work increasing and a second draft call-up looming, the company decided to take on women employees. Up until that time, they employed not a single woman, not even for office or cleaning work.

J&L would take this step carefully and deliberately. The company president, James Hartness, inventor of an advanced flat turret lathe, also had advanced ideas about industrial management. The original industrial efficiency movement, launched by Frederick W. Taylor in the 1880s, had stressed economy of motion —finding the one best way to perform a task, saving dollars by saving time. In the years leading up to the First World War, Hartness and a few other business leaders had begun to consider the human side of efficiency. The success of any machine or any business, Hartness believed, depended upon the physical and mental condition of each individual worker.[21] Output could actually be increased by dropping down to an eight-hour day, maintaining clean and bright workrooms, and carefully matching the person to the job.

Hartness wanted to hire women of "the highest type of intelligence" and to maintain "the highest social status" for the women in his shops. They would have to apply by sending a letter to the superintendent, and they would be selected according to their "fitness" for the job.[22] Drawn from the local population, these women would not be motivated by hunger, but by a desire to do precision work and to contribute to the war effort. To attract and keep such women, the company first spent three months preparing for them. A women's rest room was paneled with natural wood and decorated with dark green rugs and Mission oak furniture. A gray-haired matron, with an oak desk in the corner and a Johnson's First Aid cabinet on the wall, supervised the rest room. Nearby, in a large dressing room, each woman had her own locker and sink.

Vivian Wilson at her milling machine at Jones and Lamson. Photograph courtesy of the Springfield Art and Historical Society.

Finally, when all was ready—the job defined, the training in place, the right women chosen—the paymaster entered six new names on his books: (Mrs.) Ethel Stewart, Eugenia Spillane, Edith Raymond, Anna R. Keith, (Mrs.) Grace M. Hamlin, Carla Clarke, and Eugenia Frazier.[23] These first six began by replacing men on the hand finishing of small parts, trimming and polishing with file and emery cloth. But they quickly learned to operate milling and grinding machines, and gradually the company added more and more women. Vesta Jenks and her husband came up together from Brattleboro, where Mr. Jenks had worked in an organ factory that had to suspend operations during the war. While the husband was learning his way around a turret lathe, his wife learned to operate a Pratt and Whitney milling machine. Vivian Wilson also worked in the milling machine department making parts for the J&L turret lathes, while her husband, Arthur, worked at Springfield's other great machine tool company, Fellows Gear Shaper. By the end of the war Jones and Lamson would employ fully one hundred women in a workforce of something over seven hundred.[24]

Like the proud mechanics they worked among, the J&L women understood the value of their work and hoped they would have a future in the shops. In time they were seen visiting the company library to study such books as *How to Read a Drawing, Mechanical Engineering for Beginners,* and *Practical Calculations for Engineers.* They also formed a suffrage league and a basketball team.[25]

Literate, self-confident, well paid, and patriotic, these women could look their male coworkers in the eye and even engage in good-natured banter. In the pages of the local newspaper, Caraola M. Cram published her "Song of the Shop Girl," expressing her satisfaction with the hard work and good pay of her job at J&L. It began with the words "O happy day that fixed my choice on working in that good old shop / Through future days, I'll sing its praise, / I'll work for premium till I drop."[26]

In the next week's paper, R. B. Meyers baited her with the shop boy's reply: "O happy day, O happy day / The girls have thrown their skirts away; / I'm glad the girls have got the chance / To work like men, and wear men's pants!" But he asked if "when they land on Canaan's shore, / Will they wear pants forevermore? / Will angels there allow such things,— / As wearing pants and golden wings?"[27]

Caraola let him have it:

I do not seek to gain your praise,
For I've no bold or strident ways;
I'm just as meek as any lamb
And love to help my "Uncle Sam."
So when you get across the sea,
Just swat the kaiser one for me.
O, nothing can our spirit quench,
While earning premium on the bench.
We surely hope we're making good,
And wear the trousers as we should;
And when we reach fair Canaan's shore
To dwell in peace forevermore,
If all tradition says is true,
They will put petticoats on you.
They'll say to you in accents gay,

"You'll have to throw your pants away—
Now don't object, or say things sharp;
You've got to if you play the harp."
You'll want to play the harp and sing,
So you'll agree and join the ring;
Then you will know just how we feel,
When garbed alike we polish steel.
We don't expect to fill your place,
But better be than empty space;
And while you're at the front to fight,
We'll hustle here with all our might,
And hope when you come home some day
That we will be allowed to stay,
To work beside you right along,
And still exchange our bits of song;
And trust that on the other shore,
We'll all wear skirts forevermore.[28]

The womanalls had, indeed, caused quite a controversy in many communities. In one Indiana town, a woman's club petitioned the city council to make it illegal for women to wear their work uniforms on the street as they went to and from the factory.[29] In another factory town, an uproar occurred when women wore their overalls to a company picnic.[30] At Jones and Lamson, the subject was treated lightly, but at length, as a way of talking about men's and women's role in the war.

Warned that he might have to wear skirts in heaven, Myers replied:

I like to read your clever lays,
And would be glad to gain your praise;
I'm just a young and honest youth,
And always try to speak the truth,
And when I get across the sea,
I'll fight for you; you'll work for me.[31]

At Jones and Lamson and the other high-tech businesses of the day, as business grew, cleanliness and worker welfare improved. But in the older women's industries, change came more slowly, if at all. On September 17, fire broke out in a Newark, New Jersey, factory that made buttons for Army uniforms. The next morning's newspapers told a familiar story: an old brick building; cans of explosive button lacquer sitting about in a room with defective wiring; piles of debris blocking the exits; one narrow fire escape; overcrowded workrooms; young women jumping from windows and dying on the sidewalks; a pile of bodies found inside, crowded near a blocked exit; families struggling to identify the charred victims from a piece of jewelry or a scrap of unburned clothing. Most of the dead and injured were teenagers. The mayor launched an investigation and vowed that "if there are any death traps in the city I will drive them out."[32] Back in Springfield, Jones and Lamson added a second women's locker room and

In a speech made at the New England Manufacturers' Conference, David Earll claimed that on bevel gear cutting machines, "the slowest woman operator . . . equals the best man's day's production." The woman shown here is cutting bevel gears at a Timken axle plant. Women's Bureau photograph, courtesy of the National Archives at College Park (RG 86G-7T-2).

another lounge, decorated with wicker furniture and equipped with a new gas stove for warming coffee and cocoa at lunchtime. A second matron watched over the female workers, providing first aid and counsel.

In the pages of *American Machinist,* the editor advised his readers that "if geraniums and canaries will increase production, it is good policy to have them."[33]

■

In September, American forces launched their assault on the Saint-Mihiel salient—a bulge in the lines where the Germans had not yet been pushed back to their prewar border. Accompanying a ferocious ground attack, American Colonel Billy Mitchell commanded an air assault larger than any show of military air power ever seen. American, French, and Italian pilots severed the German line, destroyed trucks and trains, and fired across the treetops in support of American ground troops.[34] *Within four days, fifteen thousand prisoners had been taken, and the salient was entirely under Allied control.*

■

The Aircraft Industry: Buffalo, New York

Out at the end of the streetcar line, past the parklike suburbs of the city of Buffalo, the Curtiss Aeroplane and Motor Corporation had put up the largest of its factories. Within the twenty-seven-acre complex, behind the low buildings that faced the street, stood a huge glass structure that looked like an enormous greenhouse. Inside, the company built big flying boats for the Navy, and light and agile training planes for the Signal Corps.

The aircraft industry was young and new—younger than any of the people who worked in it. When the war began, only eleven years after the Wright brothers' first successful flight at Kitty Hawk, the airplane was still an experiment. It had not yet been put to work moving people or mail; it had no instruments to permit flying in bad weather; it was certainly unproven as a weapon of war. In 1914, America had only sixteen plants that made airplanes, and only 211 workers. By 1918, there were more than forty plants employing nearly 27,000 people. Of those 27,000, more than 6,000 were women; and of those 6,000, nearly 2,000 worked for Curtiss in two Buffalo plants.[35]

Inside the glass-walled factory, acres of high-ceilinged work space were divided into departments for machining, woodworking, assembling, and finishing. In an airy balcony, up above the machine tools that didn't require high ceil-

Soldering copper strips to aircraft pontoons. Women's Bureau photograph, courtesy of the National Archives at College Park (RG 86G-1H-8).

ings, a training school, staffed mostly by female teachers, trained two hundred women at a time. Other balconies housed rest rooms with couches and chairs; cloakrooms for hanging up coats, hats, and street clothes; and lavatories with rows of modern toilets and sinks. The other Curtiss factory in Buffalo, housed in an old building downtown, provided fewer comforts; but in both plants the work was light and fairly clean.

The airplane of 1918 was still largely made of wood—a spruce frame covered with heavy linen and veneer made of lightweight spruce or cedar. At the Curtiss plant, women in the woodworking shop helped shape the wooden parts, bored holes where one wing part needed to pass through another, and operated a machine that nailed wooden parts together. With bare hands and arms, women dipped the light wooden parts into varnish and hung them on a rack to dry.

Another group shaped and smoothed the propellers, then finished them with oil and varnish.

Working alongside men, women helped assemble the wing panels, the ailerons, the rudder, and the tail unit, setting the lightweight wooden pieces in place, and gluing and screwing them together. They also helped assemble the fuselage. Four long, curved beams—two upper and two lower—made up the main body of the airplane. Women assembled small wooden struts which men then used to join the beams together. After the frame of the body was built, women laid the flooring and installed the electric lights.

All of the small metal parts used to hold the wooden pieces together were also machined in the plant, mostly by women who had been trained in the com-

Assembling airplane wings. Women's Bureau photo, courtesy of the National Archives at College Park (RG 86G-1N-1).

Stitching the linen covering on airplane wings. Women's Bureau photograph, courtesy of the National Archives at College Park (RG 86G-1H-1).

In the training school at the Curtiss Aeroplane and Motor Corporation, women learned to apply dope to wings. Women's Bureau photograph, courtesy of the National Archives at College Park (RG 86G-1J-1).

pany's school. After these parts came from the cutting machines, another group of workers filed or polished them to create the exact size and surface required.

Once the airplane's frame had been assembled and the wooden veneer added to the lower parts, the wings had to be covered. First, wide strips of linen were sewn together into the rough shape of the wing. Men and women stretched the linen tightly over the wing and tacked it down. Then a crew of experienced seamstresses—many of them gray-haired alumnae of the garment industries—sewed up the loose ends of the wing covering, using heavy linen thread and large, curved darning needles. Next the wing panel was stood up on its edge, and teams of young women passed a long, three-inch darning needle back and forth,

At the Dayton-Wright Airplane Company, women assembled aircraft engines to be used in the British-built deHavilland DH-4. Women's Bureau photograph, courtesy of the National Archives at College Park (RG 86G-1K-1).

fastening the linen to the ribs, stitching it tightly to keep the fabric from flapping in the wind.

In the doping room, agile young women worked alongside the men, brushing a thick varnish onto the wings, turning the porous linen into an airtight sheath that would provide lift for the airplane. The British had already found that dope made with tetrachlorethane was poisonous,[36] and so Americans used other solvents. Still, the doping room filled up with fumes that were strong, unpleasant, and possibly hazardous. At the Curtiss plant, the doping room was shut off from the rest of the factory and—in summer at least—doors and windows to the outside were kept open.

After doping, the aircraft was ready for its final coat of paint: khaki for the Army training planes, blue-gray for the Navy's flying boats. Then women would apply the insignia from transfer paper, identifying the plane by the three concentric circles of red, white, and blue.

Throughout the plant, at each stage of the process, female inspectors checked over every part. With micrometers and calipers in hand, they made sure that each bolt and screw matched the blueprint specifications for length and width, and for the number and spacing of the threads. Where the ends of cables had been wound into place, the exact number of wraps had to be counted by inspectors. All joints and metal fittings had to be checked. The wings, ailerons, elevators, and tailpieces were inspected both before and after they were attached to the fuselage. Once the engine and gas tank had been installed, the propeller and pilot's seat put in place, and all of the cables and steering mechanisms attached, the plane was ready for packing. While a wooden crate was being built around the plane, women busily prepared the metal fittings for exposure to salt air. Each metal part had to be smeared with petroleum jelly and then wrapped with tissue paper. The smaller girls climbed up inside the plane to get to the interior metal fittings. When all was done, the lid was nailed onto the box. A sturdy derrick lifted the crate onto a waiting freight car, and the aircraft was on its way for training at the Stateside Army bases or for patrol duty along the coasts of Europe.

■

In France, American forces slowly worked their way through the Argonne forest while the French pushed northward to the River Aisne. By the end of the month, the Allies crossed the Hindenburg line—Germany's last line of defense. In the Balkans, Allied forces drove the Bulgarians across Macedonia.

■

As men continued to disappear from American factories, the need for women continued to grow. The initial draft of 1917 had called up men between the ages of twenty-one and thirty; the second draft extended the age limits to eighteen and forty-five. By the early fall of 1918, manufacturers began to realize that more trades—and more skills—would have to be opened to women. At Bethlehem Steel, the company school began to train women as all-around machinists who could read blueprints, use a variety of machines, set up their own tools, and lay

Caulking a wooden boat at the shipyard in Portsmouth, New Hampshire. According to the note on the back of the photograph, this was highly skilled work. Women's Bureau photograph, courtesy of the National Archives at College Park (RG 86G-11F-6).

out their own work.[37] In shipyards at Newark and across the country on Puget Sound, white women had begun to do carpentry and caulking.

A few black women also began to work their way out of the dirtiest jobs. Sears, Roebuck and Company, with the help of the Chicago Urban League, for the first time hired black women for clerical work in its mail-order department.[38] In Detroit, black women began to work in the auto plants as assemblers and inspectors, in the foundries as core makers, and in the munitions factories as shell makers.[39] Even in Washington, where the Wilson administration was dominated by southerners who insisted on strict racial segregation, African American women did clerical work for many government agencies. At the Bureau of Engraving, Mrs. Anna R. Grant, "an expert currency examiner," more than once worked a twenty-eight-hour shift in the crush to keep the supply of paper money up to wartime needs.[40]

Of the more than 10 million American women who worked for wages, somewhere between 1 and 2 million worked in industries directly supporting the war effort.[41] Most of them had worked even before the war—they were the child laborers photographed by Lewis Hine for the Child Labor Committee, the shirt-waist strikers of 1910 and the white-goods workers of 1911, the black share-croppers and laundresses who migrated to Chicago during the war, the meat packers, shoe workers, and shop girls who worked to support themselves and their families. They were office workers like Hutch, who now worked the night shift in a Chicago munitions plant, turning out artillery shells to send to her nephew overseas, trying to earn a man's wage to support the boy's mother and little sister while he was gone. By the fall of 1918, with nearly 4 million men in the military services and with production of weapons, ammunition, ships, and aircraft burgeoning, even the supply of working women was not enough.

Wageless Women: Bridgeport Revisited

At four o'clock in the afternoon on September 21, six military airplanes circled over Seaside Park in Bridgeport, Connecticut, dropping paper messages over the thousands of people assembled on the beach below. The wind picked up most of the leaflets and blew them out across Long Island Sound, but the band played and the crowd cheered anyway. Many in that assembly had never seen an airplane before, and this demonstration seemed like a great miracle of technology. It was also a symbol of America's growing military and industrial power, which—judg-ing from recent events in Europe—were bound to help the Allies win the war.

Some of the fifty thousand little cards drifted to the ground and into the hands of the crowd. Each card contained "A Message from the Front to the Women of Bridgeport," urging them to go to work for Uncle Sam:

> How easy it is for me to drop this message to you! And one of the Kaiser's airmen could just as easily drop a bomb, and he would in a minute if he could. The Kaiser doesn't care who he hits, old or young —women or children—they are all alike to him. That's the kind of man we are fighting. Why don't you women retaliate? You can fight at the front and live home by enlisting for pleasant easy work in the near-est munition factory. Gen. Pershing wants more men, so Uncle Sam says to you "Making munitions is woman's job—will you go to work today and hasten the end of this terrible struggle?"[42]

Which---
Will Your Brother or Sweetheart See?

Can You Imagine the Thoughts of Our Boys "Over There"—Fighting for Our Freedom—Yours and Mine—Waiting Anxiously for Food, Clothing and Ammunition? Can you sit by idly and read—lavishing in luxury, while they are perhaps languishing in pain—wounded, gassed or shell shocked?

It's Right Up to the Women Now

THEY HAVE DONE NOBLY BUT THEY MUST DO MORE, THEY MUST MAKE MUNITIONS AND WAR ESSENTIALS FOR

"MAKING MUNITIONS IS WOMAN'S JOB"

This is not a movement to reduce costs or replace men but rather a movement of expansion to supply in abundance all War Essentials —what is wanted (and right now) is women workers to produce munitions.

Women workers will be paid the same wage scale as the men for like work—and schools of instruction, which will teach the fundamentals, are being organized in the various plants to make the women workers efficient from the start.

The Work Is Easy—Pleasant—Profitable and Above All Patriotic.

Enlist Now at U. S. Employment Bureau, 303 Fairfield Ave.

Advertisement from the Bridgeport Post, *21 September 1918. Courtesy of the Connecticut State Library.*

In the following days, three thousand volunteers—the Minute Women[43]—knocked on doors all over the city, taking a census of available women and urging them to go to work. They were looking for "wageless women": middle- and upper-class women who had never worked, new college graduates waiting for their sweethearts to return from Europe so that they could be married, and mothers of young men off at the front.

Nonworking American women had already been mobilized to conserve food, plant gardens, buy war bonds, make bandages, knit for the soldiers, and do a hundred other useful womanly tasks. In Philadelphia, in a donated factory, society women volunteered their time to make clothing for European refugees. In Bridgeport, wives of the factory owners organized day nurseries for the children of immigrant women working in the local plants.[44] But not until the fall of 1918 did the federal government and local communities urge nonworking women to go into the munitions factories. Using a crude combination of insult and inspiration, newspaper articles reinforced the message of the leaflet drop: "Only those who have been the useless members of society will know the exquisite thrill of truly productive work. . . . There is nothing unpleasant about it. The big light factory rooms with the ceaseless hum of things being done are the very embodiment of the 20th century. . . . Everything here bears mute testimony to the fact that this is the army behind the men in the field."[45] The Minute Women, determined to knock on every door in the city, hoped to find twenty thousand new women willing to go into the factories.

The campaign for wageless women made the working women of Bridgeport nervous. They were in the factories to earn a living, and a sudden influx of middle-class women could drive their wages down, just when they were struggling to be taken seriously as workers.

Bridgeport was, in the fall of 1918, caught in one of the touchiest labor disputes of the war: Earlier in the summer, ten thousand Bridgeport machinists had called a strike, demanding a return to the eight-hour day established in 1916, higher wages to match the effect of inflation, and more-uniform pay scales across the city. With the machinists out, sixty thousand workers, in a total of fifty-four factories, would be unable to work, and more than half of the nation's supply of ammunition could be shut off almost overnight.[46]

As the machinists had expected, the National War Labor Board came in to negotiate a settlement that would set wages and hours for the entire city. While the board held its hearings, the machinists went back to work, and production

By the end of the war, more than ten thousand women were employed making gas masks. Whenever possible, managers hired women who had relatives serving overseas, so that the work would be done with extraordinary care. Women's Bureau photograph, courtesy of the National Archives at College Park (RG 86G-8A-8).

of ammunition continued. After several weeks of hearings, the War Labor Board announced its award, establishing a standard eight-hour day, with wage increases for all workers, and time and a half for overtime. The minimum wage for men twenty-one years of age and over would be forty-two cents an hour; for women eighteen and over, thirty-two cents.

Back in Washington, Mary Van Kleeck was outraged. The War Labor Board claimed to believe in equal pay for equal work, but by setting a lower minimum for women, it assumed that no man—however new or unskilled or obtuse—would ever be doing work at the lowest level done by women. "Following time-

The woman on the right seems to be new to the job of disassembling boxes at a salvage plant. She may have been new to the workforce altogether—one of the wageless women recruited in the last weeks of the war. Photograph courtesy of the National Archives at College Park (Signal Corps photo 111-SC-26300).

honored precedent," she complained, "they admit sex as a basis for wage-fixing."[47] She wrote to Major Tully at the War Department urging that he find a way to impose a wage increase for women at the Remington plants doing government work, as a supplement to the War Labor Board's award.[48]

The machinists were no happier with their own part of the settlement, because it still failed to fix uniform wages across the city, and so they called another strike.[49] Finally, on September 13, President Wilson intervened. Labeling the strike disloyal and dishonorable, he threatened to bar the strikers from work in any war industry and to have their draft exemptions removed.[50] When some employers refused to take the strikers back, the president threatened to seize control of the factories. Within days, the machinists were back at work, while the War Labor Board began to review its decision. Thus the government created some balance between the power of the employers and the power of the machinists' union.

In the midst of this crisis, Bridgeport's working women resolved to increase their own power. Faced with an ever-increasing demand for female labor that could only be filled—and might soon become filled—by middle- and upper-class women, they knew they must act to unite the women of the city. On the very day of the leaflet drop over Seaside Park, a group of seventy-five women met at the machinists' headquarters and voted to organize a women's union, open to any woman—skilled or unskilled—employed in any factory in Bridgeport.[51] With a strong union, they hoped to be able to demand equal pay in fact, not just in theory. They received approval for a charter from the AFL and promises of help from leaders of the machinists' union, who had finally realized that unorganized women could threaten only their own wages.

Meanwhile, the Minute Women launched their campaign. In the first week after the leaflet drop, they interviewed 15,000 women. Thirteen hundred pledged to go to work full-time, and within eleven days, 1,000 of them had been placed in jobs. Another 3,200 agreed to work part-time.[52] The numbers, however, were disappointing: the Minute Women were falling far short of their goal. They opened more day nurseries to serve working-class mothers, and held more rallies to attract middle-class women. Margaret Wilson, the president's daughter, came up from Washington for one meeting.[53] But most of the women who wanted to work had gone into the factories months before. The rest would need more time, or more compelling recruitment.

■

Bulgaria surrendered on the last day of September. In early October, the Germans began to ask for an armistice, but the Allies demanded a surrender. President Wilson, who still hoped to end the war with the plan outlined in his Fourteen Points, nonetheless insisted that America could not negotiate with a military dictatorship. The Allies continued their attacks, taking prisoners and guns at every turn.

■

When the War Labor Board published its revised ruling in early October, it reemphasized that women doing the same work as men should be paid the same wage. It also, however, pointed out the need to pay a woman a lower wage when she required extra help.[54] Leaving the women's minimum wage below the men's, the board still refused to admit that the lowest skilled man might be worth as little as the lowest skilled woman. On this one issue, Mary Van Kleeck, and the working women of Bridgeport, would never get through to the men on the board.

By mid-October, Bridgeport began to realize that the war would soon end and the country would not need thousands of married middle- and upper-class women in the munitions factories. Then the great Spanish flu epidemic hit Bridgeport, and the Minute Women shifted their efforts from recruiting factory workers to registering volunteer nurses. The munitions recruiting campaign ended just as it was beginning.

The two groups of women—the working and the wageless—would not be meeting one another on the shop floor. Middle-class women would not be abandoning their traditional feminine roles; and laboring women, though their dreams of a citywide union faded away, would continue to see themselves less as symbols of patriotism than as workers—female workers—struggling to earn a living.

■

On October 30 Turkey surrendered, and on November 3 the Austrians signed an armistice with Italy. As news of German negotiations with Woodrow Wilson reached the German troops and the German people, mutinies and revolts overthrew the government. On November 9, Kaiser Wilhelm abdicated and fled the country, while a German delegation continued negotiations with the Allied commander. At 11:00 A.M. Paris time, on the eleventh day of the eleventh month, 1918, all firing ceased.

■

The armistice celebration in Springfield, Vermont. Photograph courtesy of the Springfield Art and Historical Society (misc. 560).

In Springfield, Vermont, five thousand joyful people gathered in the town square. Amid a cacophony of firecrackers, whistles, and drums, the flag-waving crowd "forgot all about being calm and collected," according to a local reporter, "and completely lost control of their New England reserve." Another two thousand citizens assembled in a mile-long parade, headed by a marshal on horseback. Behind him came the Springfield Concert Band and the Red Cross women in their white caps and aprons. The veterans of the Civil War rode on trucks, and another truck carried a mock kaiser's coffin, with someone dressed as Uncle Sam nailing down the lid. Five hundred schoolchildren marched in front of the men of the fire department, who were in dress uniform. Local carpenters and foundry men took their place in the parade to demonstrate their contributions to the war effort, while power company trucks and decorated cars and a tank made of cardboard filled in among the marchers. At the head of the Bryant Grinder Company marched thirty-seven women from the machine shop, and the women from the Jones and Lamson shops carried a banner announcing that they were one hundred strong. However integrated into the workforce they may have become, they were still, according to their banner, "women war workers."

In the town square, the revelers burned the kaiser in effigy. Then there were speeches, music, a prayer, and more speeches. When the band played "Keep the Home Fires Burning," the crowd sang along. The celebration ended after dark, with the playing of "The Star-Spangled Banner."

Only eleven days earlier, Caraola Cram had published another poem, which included her hopes for the future:

I'm glad you are a model youth,
For it would grieve my soul;
To sit up there and play the harp,
And watch you shovel coal;
And if you help along the cause,
With all your might and strength;
I'm confident you'll get your skirts,
And of the proper length.
Just get the kaiser on the job,
And then come back to me;
And we will work here side by side,
As happy as can be.[55]

CHAPTER SEVEN

Demobilized: Streetcars and Railroads, 1918-1919

THE FIRST LAYOFFS CAME swiftly. As soon as the armistice was signed, women on the night shift at the Frankford Arsenal were let go. By November 14, Curtiss Aeroplane had discharged three thousand people. In Bridgeport, the Remington–Union Metallic Cartridge company announced plans to release up to half of its workforce. Fifteen machine shops in Worcester, Massachusetts, had by late December laid off more than twelve hundred women, and expected to release the rest of them as soon as the war contracts were finished.[1]

In other industries, change came less quickly. Two million American men were still in Europe and would take many months to come home. In the Stateside training camps and in the factories, a great influenza epidemic was killing thousands of Americans per week. And so in the secondary war industries, women would hold onto their jobs a bit longer. Meatpackers still had to send food to the troops in Europe. Machine tools, once again needed for making consumer goods, were still in short supply. At Jones and Lamson, James Hartness called a meeting to

Laborers at Busch terminal in Brooklyn, New York. Women's Bureau photograph, courtesy of the National Archives at College Park (RG 86G-6T-1).

assure the women that the company still needed them, and so Caraola Cram continued to work beside the shop boys for a time.[2] On the railroads, too, women's departure would be slow, and sometimes painful.[3] Florence Clark, a field agent for the U.S. Railroad Administration, had been hired to protect them; she would instead be watching them go.

In the early twentieth century, railroads formed the primary transport network throughout the country. During the war, trains not only moved troops, weapons, and ammunition; they also carried raw materials for the foundries and factories, coal for the power plants, and food for the army and the nation's hungry allies in Europe. By late 1917, the railroads had been nearly paralyzed by insufficient coordination, corporate shortsightedness, and labor strife. The confusion left cargo stranded at supply points. Freight cars full of supplies bound for Europe stood unloaded at the East Coast docks.[4] Then in December 1917, in order to keep war materials moving, the government had taken control. Under a single administration, freight began to move more rationally. Likewise, labor conflicts were more readily resolved. The Railroad Administration established wage increases, employment standards, and a basic eight-hour day.

From the beginning of the war, the number of women on the railroads had grown steadily until, by November 1918, there were seventy thousand more women railroad workers than there had been in 1917.[5] From Maine to Florida to Kansas to Oregon, they were working in the offices, on the track repair crews, in the machine shops, and in the rail yards. To provide some protection for these new workers, the administration formed the Women's Service Section in August and brought in Pauline Goldmark, of the New York Consumers' League, as manager.[6] In early October she hired four field agents. Although the war ended within a few weeks, the Railroad Administration continued its work. The nation's railroads still needed women's labor, and the women certainly still needed their jobs.

The Women's Service Section was charged with seeing that they had safe working conditions and fair wages, including "the same rate of pay as men for the same class of work."[7] The administration made it clear that equal pay for women was not necessarily a recognition of equal ability, just as equal pay for black firemen and trainmen was "not to be interpreted as a recognition of social equality." The principle of equal pay would simply keep employers from hiring blacks and women at lower wages when white men were available.[8] Such, anyway, was the stated opinion of the men in charge. The agents of the Women's

Service Section, however, interpreted their jobs in their own way. And they were the ones out in the field inspecting rail yards and pressuring people to follow the rules. In their first three months, the four field agents conducted 407 inspections in eleven states and the District of Columbia.[9]

Florence Clark had the right temperament for the work. Twenty-eight years old, she was confident and outspoken, even brash in the face of resistance from railroad managers and union officials. She asked probing questions about hours and wages, examined rest-room facilities, talked with union leaders, watched the

Cleaning up after track repair on the Erie Railroad. Sometimes entire families worked in the rail yards, living in boxcar communities. Women's Bureau photograph, courtesy of the National Archives at College Park (RG 86G-6T-9).

women work, and—when necessary—demanded cooperation in the name of the federal government.

Clark had been educated at the University of Chicago, which had a strong tradition of progressive social reform, and had come to her railroad job straight from the Children's Bureau of the Department of Labor, where she had served as an investigator, traveling through the Carolinas, facing down frequent hostility to the new federal child labor law.[10] Now, inspecting conditions in the rail yards, she brought to her work a maternal protectionism typical of middle-class reformers. Women who had been exploited in the garment sweatshops and the laundries could just as easily be exploited by the railroads, and Clark had been assigned to look after them. To the women who worked for the railroads, earning higher wages and working shorter hours than ever before, she brought help and—it would turn out—disappointment.

She spent late October and early November studying the Baltimore yards of the B&O Railroad, beginning with the Bailey yards at the foot of Utah Street.[11] There she found black women who had been cleaning the insides of cars for twelve years and who had, sometime during the past summer, walked out and refused to work unless their wages were increased to meet their rapidly rising cost of living. Local managers had brought the women back the next day, with a raise of three-fourths of a cent per hour, to thirty-three cents. To Florence Clark, this was not good enough, and she applied pressure to get them raised to thirty-five cents—the wage paid to men cleaners working for the Pullman Company and to white women working directly for the B&O Railroad. She also tried to hurry along plans to build them a new rest room and an indoor toilet in place of the toilet in a shed out in the yard, which they shared with the men, and which tended to freeze up in the winter.

At the Bailey yards, and the next day at the Riverside yards, Clark also saw women who had more recently been hired to clean the outsides of cars. Using ladders or long-handled brushes, they washed the coaches and the coal tenders and all of the windows. Before they cleaned the engines, men sprayed on a black, oily liquid called Modoc. Then women in overalls climbed up onto the engine to wipe it off with rags. Women swept the tracks and picked up stray pieces of coal. In repair yards, they picked up scrap lumber and metal, piled it into wheelbarrows, and trundled their loads to the scrap heap.

At the Riverside yard, Clark also came across her first case of a skilled worker deliberately denied the wages given to men doing the same work. Mary

Engine wipers in Great Falls, Montana. War Department photograph, courtesy of the National Archives at College Park (165-WW-595D [14]).

Linthicum had come to the repair shop at Riverside in June 1917 and, for a couple of weeks, worked at simply cleaning brake valves that came in for repair. By the fall of 1918, Linthicum was both testing and repairing valves: running eight different tests, renewing cylinder cap gaskets, and grinding in the check valves. Still she was making only thirty-five cents an hour—about the same as a common laborer in the yards.

When Florence Clark arrived to look over the situation at Riverside, Mary Linthicum lost no time in registering a complaint. She had tried, she said, to join the union, but was told that "no women are allowed." Without union support, she could do nothing about her wages. Clark began exploring the situation and found, in the same shop, a friendly and sympathetic valve repairman, Mr. Schreiber, who agreed that Linthicum should be getting fifty cents an hour, but warned that most of the men were against allowing her any such wage. In fact, he told her confidentially, when the wage adjustments had been made, the shop's master mechanic and the union's shop committee together had decided "to permit Mrs. Linthicum to work in the shop," but agreed she would be paid only thirty-five cents per hour. The general master mechanic for Baltimore happened to be at the Riverside yards that day, and Clark found him receptive. A week later, he sent Clark a letter reporting that Mary Linthicum had begun receiving 48½ cents an hour, and would receive back pay for the time when she was misclassified.

With the Mary Linthicum case, Florence Clark also confronted the third part of her charge from the Women's Service Section. Not only was she to ensure that women received the same wages as men for the same class of work, and that sanitary and comfort facilities were provided to women working in male-dominated environments; she was also to consider whether women's new railroad work was "suited to their strengths and aptitudes," and if necessary have them removed from overly heavy tasks or unsuitable working conditions.[12] Finding that Mary Linthicum had to lift valves weighing up to sixty pounds, Clark reported that "there is a grave question whether women should be permitted to go on this kind of work." She suggested that at least there should be a physical exam for women before they could become valve testers. Mary Linthicum, however, could obviously handle the job, and so she was left in peace.

Women doing common labor in rail yards around the country were not being left in peace. When muscle power was cheaper than gasoline power, "truckers" piled heavy loads of freight into large carts or wagons and pulled them—like the European peasant pulling a plow—from the freight house to a train, or from the train to the freight house. The work was heavy—too heavy for women, in the opinion of W. G. McAdoo, the director general of railroads. In September, while men were still being shipped abroad at the rate of thousands every day, McAdoo had asked that women be removed from all work as section hands and truckers for the railroads.[13] Helen Ross, another young field agent with the Women's Service Section, had to check on compliance on the Santa Fe Railroad in Kansas City, Missouri.

Women had been hired to pull trucks in Kansas City the summer before, when the warehouse had 450 freight cars backed up waiting to be unloaded. The foreman spread the word among the black men in the yards that black women would be hired, and before long he had eighty-five women on the job, pulling heavy loads to and from the freight cars. There were still some men working as truckers, too, and when the women showed up, men who had been moving only 1,300 pounds each hour began to move more than 1,700 pounds. The women carried slightly less in each load but worked steadily, averaging 1,682 pounds an hour. Then came the order from the director general, and gradually women were replaced with men whenever men could be found.

In the fall, Helen Ross watched the remaining twenty-one women truckers and talked to them about their work. All of them, they said, had done harder work before, as housecleaners or laundry workers. The trucks were neatly balanced, they claimed, and their arms had quickly become accustomed to the pulling. More important, the hours were shorter and the pay higher in the freight yard than anywhere else they had worked. The youngest of the women, twenty-one-year-old Pearl Jones, told Ross, "All the colored women like this work and want to keep it. . . . What occupation is open to us where we can make really good wages? We are not employed as clerks, we can not all be school teachers. . . . Of course we should like easier work than this if it were opened to us, but this pays well and is no harder than other work open to us. With three dollars a day, we can buy bonds to take care of us in our old age, we can dress decently, and not be tempted to find our living on the streets. . . . The only time our work is heavy is when we have to pull the trucks over a bad place on the platform but the men are always good to help. Please don't take this work away from us."[14]

Helen Ross, a gentle soul, wanted to find a way to let the women keep their jobs. In her report back to Washington, she suggested that the director general's rule might be too broad. "A study might be made with the view to working out a

Before the war, women's work was restricted not simply by their supposed weakness, but by the clothes that respectable women wore. Women's Bureau photograph, courtesy of the National Archives at College Park (RG 86G-6T-2).

code of rulings regarding the use of women as truckers, to safeguard the health and welfare of the women," she wrote. No such code would be developed, however, and with the war ending it would soon become easier to find men for the work.[15]

Shoveling scrap metal on a rail yard truck, on the Baltimore & Ohio Railroad, at Glenwood, Pennsylvania. Women's Bureau photograph, courtesy of the National Archives at College Park (RG 86G-6T-6).

Back in Baltimore, Florence Clark noticed a change in the rail yards as soon as the armistice was signed.[16] In October, the general superintendent at the Mount Clare shops of the B&O had praised the women in his yard, saying that their work was as good as the men's. Suddenly, after November 11, he took on a disparaging tone. He would, it seemed, be glad to be rid of them. The storekeeper, Mr. Johnson, was openly hostile. He had under him a group of white women who had been laid off as truckers and brought inside to do clerical work—an option not available to the black women in Kansas City. Classified as storeroom attendants, these women actually spent most of their time keeping records, checking prices, tracing orders, and following shipments. Johnson complained that the women now had the easiest work in the office and he refused to call them clerks. Clerks, according to the railroad classifications, would have to receive 42½ cents an hour, and if he paid 42½ cents to women "for writing," his men would quit. The regulations, however, were clear. When Clark referred the matter to the B&O's general storekeeper, the women were reclassified and paid as clerks.

At the Mount Clare shops Clark also met, for the first time, women welders, drill press operators, and blacksmith's helpers. She was especially struck by the determination and imagination of the electric arc welders. Before taking up welding, one woman had been a weaver, another a spinner. The rest had worked as a telephone operator, a button inspector, a cashier, a sewing machine operator, a cigarette maker, and so on. There were fifteen women in all—ten of them under twenty-one and only one over thirty. Outside in the repair yard, three or four other women did oxyacetylene welding, lugging their sixty-five-pound tanks of oxygen and acetylene around the yard to get close to the work.

The most accomplished and outspoken of the electric welders, nineteen-year-old Burton Gaither, had been welding for more than a year. Before that, she had worked as a timekeeper, earning only eight dollars each week. Now she was earning fifty cents an hour and bonuses for piecework. When the shop foreman first put her on welding, Burton could get none of the men to train her. She experimented until she learned to make the molten metals flow together just right, and learned to adjust the protective screen so she would not hurt her eyes. Lying awake at night, she figured out how to hold her tools so that she would not get burned. Sometimes the men in the shop would come over and begin working on the same piece, welding and riveting uncomfortably close, trying to frighten the women away. When the men found that the women would not be

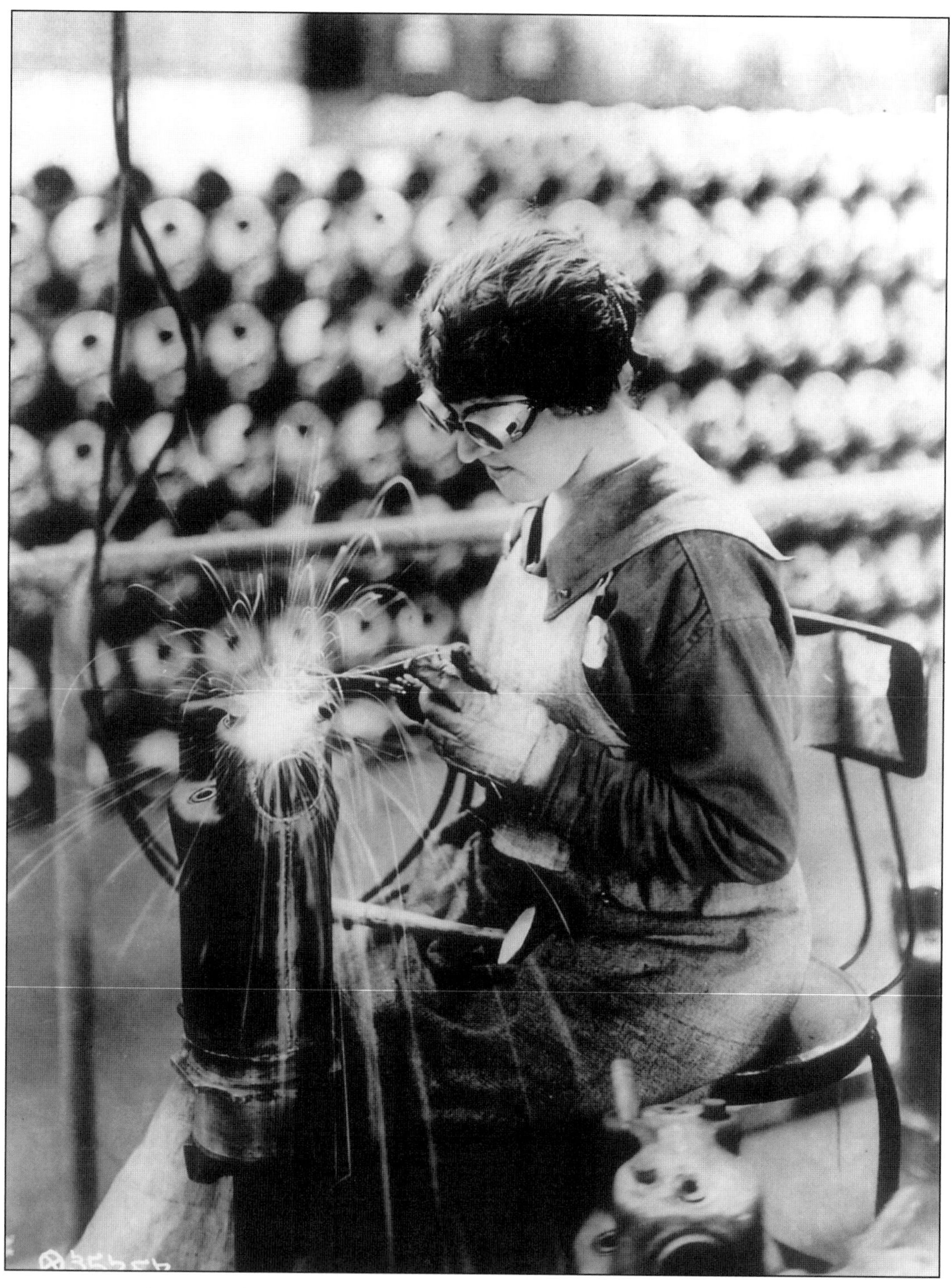

An oxyacetylene welder working on a water jacket for an aircraft engine. Photograph courtesy of the National Archives at College Park (Signal Corps photo 35757).

driven off, they began to refuse to work with them. One day in August, Gaither had been working inside a boiler, while two men had been assigned to work on the outside. Suddenly the shop foreman came around and called to her, "Burton, come off the job you are on!" She wasn't allowed back on that job for a week, until the men were finished, because they had refused to work alongside her. Still, she stuck with the job, and she earned ninety-six dollars for her thirteen days on boiler work.

By the time Florence Clark inspected the Mount Clare shop, Burton Gaither had already convinced the management to set up a screen inside the door of the women's dressing room, thus ensuring their privacy when someone opened the door, and to install a bell that the foreman could ring if he wanted to come into the dressing room. Burton was also training new women as welders, on her own time. But she had not been able to join the union or get for herself the appropriate wage for a second-year craftsman.

Just as the war was about to end, the men at the Mount Clare shops had begun to talk of letting the women into the union. They were feeling a bit more comfortable with the women, and were beginning to fear for their own wages. If the war ended and government control ceased, nonunion women working at low wages could drive the men's pay down. But when Florence Clark visited, the men were still just talking about a union for women and were insisting that the women would have to organize their own, separate local.

When Clark wrote her report on the Mount Clare shops, she recommended wage increases for the women welders and suggested several comfort and safety measures. She was convinced, however, that the Women's Service Section had much more to do there. The management could not be trusted to give the women fair play, and the union men would give them support only when it served their own self-interest. Many of the jobs, too, posed a familiar problem. Welding seemed such a wonderful opportunity for women—it demanded skill and imagination, and it paid well. And yet it also required heavy lifting and sitting on cold floors to reach the lower parts of objects too large to go on a bench. Blacksmith work, too, offered high wages, but exposed women to noxious fumes and physical strain. Then there was "Big Alice," a burly woman who had proven that she could toss lumber into cars as well as any man, but who—if put on as supervisor of other women—might set an impossible and unhealthy pace. Not yet willing to let the Burton Gaithers of the world take care of themselves, Florence Clark reported that the Women's Service Section would need, espe-

Common labor work in a rail yard. Women's Bureau photograph, courtesy of the National Archives at College Park (RG 86G-6T-5).

cially, to study the work of women welders, to decide "whether to develop this field for women or shut them out of it all together."

In late November, Florence Clark was in Minnesota, delivering bad news to a group of women truckers.[17] The foreman, Mr. Fullerton, wanted to keep the women because they were much more reliable than the men who were available. Any man in St. Paul with strength, brains, skill, or a strong work ethic was either still in the army or in a better job than loading and pulling freight trucks. The women, according to their forewoman, liked their jobs, needed the money, and wanted to stay. Clark, however, saw her duty clearly. The director general had given his order, and the women must be removed.

She met with them during their noon lunch break on December 2. They assembled in the women's dressing room—twenty-five women truckers, their forewoman, the attendant who looked after the dressing room, and Mr. Kleiber, a representative of the Brotherhood of Railway Clerks. Kleiber was anxious to have Clark assure the women that their removal had nothing to do with the union. She explained that the order was general, and that women pulling trucks in rail yards across the country were being transferred or laid off. The Minnesota Transfer Company, a small belt line, had no other positions available, but the superintendent would to try to find them jobs as car cleaners on other lines. Clark herself had been to the local office of the U.S. Employment Service to arrange for the women to have help in finding new jobs. To Clark's surprise, the women protested very little, asked polite questions, and seemed confident that they would find other work.

Perhaps they had not yet seen the newspaper ads that were now reading "Wanted—Women. At pre-war wages."[18] In the end, a few of the married women at Minnesota Transfer decided they no longer needed to work. The Employment Service placed seventeen of the others. Just before Christmas, Florence Clark heard that many of them were now working for twelve dollars a week—about half of what they had earned hauling freight for the railroad.

■

In early December, President Wilson and a large entourage sailed from New York to attend the peace conference in Paris. In January, the victors of the Great War met to negotiate among themselves the terms of the peace.

■

By early winter, the railroads were ready to reduce their workforce. Although the Railroad Administration had actively worked to remove women from truck pulling and track repair work, the officials had no intention of allowing women in lighter jobs to be targeted in the coming layoffs. Orders went out that the force reduction should be done strictly by seniority and that current workers should be transferred to available jobs before anyone new could be hired. Men who had left railroad jobs to find better-paying work in munitions plants would have no right to return and displace the women. Only returning soldiers would take precedence. Florence Clark and Helen Ross would spend most of the coming year monitoring compliance with this order, and witnessing, in spite of their efforts, the gradual dismissal of women from the railroads.

In the Harrisburg yards of the Pennsylvania Railroad, trouble was first stirred up by a group of male employees who wrote an anonymous letter to William Elmer, acting superintendent of the yards. "Now that the war is over and the men are trying to find work," they wrote, "give the men the jobs. . . . Our men came first before the war, why not now? Women help ought to be entirely taken off the railroad." Apparently the management in Harrisburg agreed, because women began to be discharged quickly—not just outdoor laborers, but storeroom attendants and clerks. Florence Clark was on the spot immediately, and she met with strong resistance: seniority lists were withheld, and women were discouraged from talking to her. She managed, however, to demonstrate

In the Navy Yard at Puget Sound, as in rail yards around the country, women worked in supply rooms for the first time. Women's Bureau photograph, courtesy of the National Archives at College Park (RG 86G-7A-33).

that the women had been let go wholesale, without regard for seniority, and that records had been altered to make it look as though the women had been fired for incompetence. When Clark brought the whole matter before Pauline Goldmark and, through her, before the director general of the railroads, the women were reinstated.[19]

In mid-April, the women storeroom attendants were given thirty days to prove that they could perform their duties. They would find it surprisingly difficult. Florence Bowen quickly learned that the work at her desk had tripled and that she also had new duties out in the yard. Within days, she and two other women had quit. Mrs. Snyder stayed longer, putting up with harder physical labor and with being snubbed by the men in the storehouse, who would not answer her simple questions.[20] Cora Knisely, who supported herself and her blind mother, was required to climb ladders all day, bringing heavy items down from high shelves. During the war, the heavier part of the storeroom duties had been performed by men. Now, the women were expected to lift brake shoes and valves that weighed up to seventy pounds.[21] When Cora lost her nerve and refused to bring material down from a top shelf, she received a formal reprimand. In mid-May, she wrote to Florence Clark saying that she had been treated "like a beast" but would not give up. Annie Lingle found herself reassigned to a dark cellar, but she, too, needed the work and wanted to hang on.[22] Within another week, Anna Crosson, a clerk in the freight office, reported to Clark that both Knisely and Lingle—the last two women storeroom attendants—were gone.[23] Crosson, too, suffered insult and harassment, but still had her job in the office.

The same thing happened in the Mount Vernon shop of the Pennsylvania Railroad, where women who had worked as outdoor laborers were first laid off, then recalled. Suddenly they found themselves loading large pieces of scrap iron, lifting barrels, and shoveling coal all day, while men more recently hired were doing the lighter work that the women had done before. When the women filed a complaint, the local master mechanic defended the changed procedures in the yard. With the reduction in workforce, he claimed, it was no longer possible to separate the lighter work from the heavy work. When the Railroad Administration reviewed the complaint, the women were overruled. Unable to meet the new demands of their jobs, they drifted away from rail yard work.[24]

Women were not, however, being driven disproportionately from all railroad jobs. They became firmly established as telephone and telegraph operators. Many women clerks kept their jobs, too, in spite of the efforts of male clerks to drive them out. Clerical work held little interest for returning soldiers or for men who had passed the last two years earning fabulous wages in the munitions plants, and so the need for female clerks remained. Work traditionally done by women, such as cleaning the inside of Pullman cars and sorting and counting the linens, also remained their own.

There was a relentless falling off, though, of women in nontraditional jobs on the railroads. Driven out of the heaviest work by good-intentioned reformers and out of the most desirable work by hostile union men and indifferent supervisors, twenty thousand women left the railroads in the year following end of the war. Though some must have left happily, many others shared the feelings expressed in a letter written by Carrie B. Fearing, a laborer who lost her job to a man in January of 1919:

> [I]f our work was satisfactory why not let us stay[?] what matters who does it so it is done and done right? . . . We are women that needed the work very much. [O]ne woman gave her only support to the army[,] one has her aged Father[,] another has a small son and I supported my disabled Sister . . . while her son was in the service of U.S.A. and if we are good enough to do the work in the last year we are good enough to do it yet. We never took a soldiers place, a soldier would not do the work we did . . . sweeping, picking up waste & paper and hauling steel shavings. . . . We are of which I speak respectable but poor women and were liked and respected by all who knew us. . . . Women's work is so very hard to find this time of year and expences are so high with Liberty bonds and insurence to pay and home expences it is hard to get by . . . it matters little who does the work so long as it is done right[.] [W]e would not do it if we did not need it.[25]

■

In March of 1919, as details of the peace treaty were being negotiated in Paris, thirty-seven United States senators issued a statement declaring that Wilson's proposed League of Nations would be unacceptable to America.

■

While women were gradually being driven from their railroad jobs, Laura Prince struggled to hold on as a streetcar conductor in Cleveland.[26] She had worked for

Operating a crossing gate. Women's Bureau photograph, courtesy of the National Archives at College Park (RG 86G-6T-3).

A streetcar conductor at work. Women's Bureau photograph, courtesy of the National Archives at College Park (RG 86G-11C-2).

ten years as a waitress, in any one day walking ten miles and carrying fifteen hundred pounds of food and dishes. During the second summer of the war, when the Cleveland Street Railway Company could not find enough men to take tickets and keep records on the streetcars, she had answered their newspaper ad and become a conductor. Compared to waitressing, it was a dream job.[27]

After 170 women were hired, the male conductors objected. The work, they claimed, was unsuitable for women, and the women, they feared, would weaken their union. They threatened a strike that would shut down the city's entire streetcar system. From the Department of Labor in Washington, two representatives hurried to Cleveland to investigate the crisis. When they reported finding no real labor shortage in Cleveland, the Secretary of Labor—apparently without consulting Mary Anderson and Mary Van Kleeck—recommended that the women conductors be dismissed in order to keep the Cleveland streetcars, and Cleveland businesses, running.

The women protested immediately. Supported by the Woman in Industry Service and the Women's Trade Union League, they appealed to the National War Labor Board, which agreed to consider the case in early December and ordered that the women be kept on until after the hearing. Now came the men's turn to protest. On December 3, 1918, they called a strike that did indeed shut down the city's main transportation system. When Cleveland's mayor asked for a quick decision in favor of the men, the NWLB issued its recommendation: the Cleveland Street Railway Company should "employ no more women for this service and . . . within the next thirty days they shall replace the present force of women by competent men."[28]

In Cleveland and around the country, women rallied immediately, urging that the case be reopened. Mary Van Kleeck and Mary Anderson wrote to the board complaining that the government must not order dismissal of "an entire group of women" simply "as a means of settling an industrial dispute."[29] From the headquarters of the National Women's Trade Union League came a letter calling the decision "unjust, undemocratic and un-American . . . and . . . a denial of the elementary right to work." Among the ten signatures were the names of Margaret Dreier Robins, Rose Schneiderman, Fannia Cohn, and Agnes Nestor.[30] The board agreed to rehear the case.[31]

In March 1919, when Laura Prince finally got to speak before the National War Labor Board, she answered every argument ever given for keeping women off the streetcars. To the criticism that the work was too difficult for women, she

At the end of the war, the Brooklyn Rapid Transit Company fired nearly three hundred women, citing the state law that prohibited women's night work. War Department photograph, courtesy of the National Archives at College Park (165-WW-595-E-13).

answered that it was far easier than waiting tables, which had begun to weaken her health. To the criticism that the work exposed women to insult and to traveling through the city late at night, she pointed out that women who wait tables or clean in hotels often work until one in the morning, and that a woman working on the public cars is protected from insult by the very presence of the public. To the criticism that women should leave jobs for men who have families to support, she explained that she had two sons to support, aged nine and eleven, while her husband was still in the service in Germany. And to the criticism that the presence of women would weaken the union, she presented evidence that she had tried to join the union—so as not to undermine it—but had been refused.

Mary Van Kleeck could not be present, but she sent a long telegram. There could be, she said, "no more critical issue in labor problems . . . before the country at this moment than to give women freedom to choose their occupation. In the war the extension of their activity was required for the nation and they responded to the need and proved their ability. For the sake of the millions of homes in which the income is largely or wholly contributed by women, the opportunities for employment must not be restricted on the grounds of preventing competition with men. . . . Favorable decision in this case will give women freedom to contribute their best energies to the industry of the nation in peace as they have done in war." Other speakers asserted that the women were not taking the places of any returning soldiers: even in the spring of 1919, there were still unfilled places for conductors in Cleveland. The women's attorney, Frank Walsh, argued that the work was largely clerical and entirely safe, that the women could not be considered strikebreakers because they had tried their best to join the union, and that the women had not had a chance to be heard before the earlier decision was made.

The most eloquent testimony came from Dr. Anna Howard Shaw, a physician, an ordained minister, and one of the most respected leaders of the woman suffrage movement. Shaw had spent the entire nineteen months of the war rallying and organizing women for the war effort, from her position as chair of the Woman's Committee of the Council of National Defense. A silver-haired woman with an imposing presence, she stood up to speak, as was her custom when she spoke from the pulpit or at a suffrage rally.

> Is it not astonishing, gentlemen, that women are not quite as interested in their own moral conditions as men can be for them, and is it not quite remarkable that women may not know what kind of employments they are adapted to as well as men can tell them? . . . Let me say that the time has come when it is neither the right of men nor the duty of men nor justice for men to decide these problems for women . . . let us be tested by our act to render good service and our act to be faithful in that service. If we fail then, let us fail, but do not let us fail by the direction of men or by the direction of any group of people. . . . So I am simply here to make a plea not for the women of the street car organization but for all womanhood, and while we are fighting for justice for Belgium

> and France and Russia and Germany, let us grant a little of it to the toiling women of our own country who responded without conscription to every demand made upon them by their Government.[32]

Given his turn to speak, the attorney for the streetcar union could do little but argue that the War Labor Board had no jurisdiction in the case. His argument failed to persuade, and the board ordered that the women be reinstated. The men's streetcar union, however, refused to accept the decision, and threatened to strike again if any women were brought back on. With the war over, the National War Labor Board had lost both its moral authority and the power to enforce its rulings. And so the Cleveland Railway Company, now fearing the conductors more than it feared an emasculated arbitration board in Washington, refused to reinstate the women. Laura Prince, banned from her local waitresses' union because it was headed by the same man who ran the local streetcar union, would have to find new work, as would the other sixty-three women who had hung onto their conductor jobs to the last.

■

On June 28, 1919, the Paris Peace Conference ended with the signing of a treaty that included Woodrow Wilson's controversial League of Nations, along with heavy punishment for Germany, including the destruction of its navy, the loss of significant territory, and an order to pay the Allies the full cost of the war. Wilson's dream of an international body that could peacefully settle disputes would die at the hands of party politics and American isolationism. The new distribution of power in Europe would leave the continent as unstable as ever and the world no more "safe for democracy" than it had been before the war.

■

The war was over; the war jobs were gone. The gradual dismissal of women from railroad work was simply a protracted version of what happened to women in other industries around the country; and the streetcar conductors were simply the most visible among women struggling to keep jobs that had allowed them, for a time, to escape from the underpaid and often unhealthy female trades.

The interlude had lasted only two years—two years of steady employment without fear of seasonal layoffs; two years of wages that could feed a young woman living on her own; two years of hoping for, and often getting, training for a new job; two years of demanding and securing rest rooms and cafeterias and clinics. The women had also spent two years caught in the crossfire between angry work-

Poor women's food riot in New York. Photograph courtesy of the National Archives at College Park (Signal Corps photo 111-SC-044813).

men and manipulative employers. And during the last year of the war, when women's labor seemed necessary to victory, they had earned praise from the press and from government agencies, and congratulations for doing a man's job. In 1919, the applause ended and the criticism grew more strident. The bosses, the men in the shops, the press, and many of the people in government expected women to return to their prewar occupations. Some of them went willingly; others protested loudly. All of them faced stress and change, for the year 1919 did not bring an era of domestic peace or a sense of comfortable normalcy.

Peace in Europe brought only new turmoil at home. The government mediators and labor boards that had forced cooperation and compromise during the war now closed up their offices. Congress did authorize continuation of the Woman in Industry Service, now called the Women's Bureau, but in peacetime the bureau would have even less authority than during the war, and would come to focus on research, advocacy, and education.

Free of government intervention, labor and management resumed their prewar struggle. Industrial leaders began antiunion campaigns and resumed the practice of firing union organizers. Several northeastern textile companies moved their plants to the South, where wages were lower and unions weaker.[33] In some of the large cities, child labor and industrial home work persisted, while the candy factories, laundries, and restaurants still paid wages too low to support a woman living alone.[34]

Meanwhile, workers, hoping to build on wartime gains, staged more than three thousand strikes over the course of the year. Food shortages and high prices continued after the war, fueling workers' discontent. In January 1919, poor women from New York's East Side tenement districts staged a protest over high food prices. They overturned food pushcarts and marched to City Hall to complain to the mayor. The food riots, like the strikes, brought little change.

For black women, the loss of war jobs was made more painful by racial violence. In Chicago, while food orders from Europe dwindled and white soldiers began to return home, black migrants continued to arrive spontaneously from the South. By early May more than ten thousand black laborers were looking for work in the city, while gangs of Irish ruffians roamed the streets, menacing the entire black community. Then on a Sunday afternoon in late July, a small group of black youths strayed into the water off a whites-only beach. When they were pelted with stones, one boy drowned; and when a police officer refused to make any arrests, the city erupted into violence.[35] Thirteen days of rioting left fifteen whites and twenty-three blacks dead, and countless homes and shops burned to the ground.

When black workers finally returned to the stockyards, escorted by armed troops, the gulf between black workers and the stockyard unions had widened.[36] At a Chicago tannery, black women who had stayed away from their jobs during the riot came back to find their places filled by white girls. The employer, believing that black women and white women would not work together, decided not to take the black women back.[37] Similar race riots in other cities—both North and South—intensified the struggle of black women workers, most of whom worked in white homes or white-run businesses.

In the 1920s, women bobbed their hair and bared their arms, but many of them returned to the traditional female trades in textile mills and garment factories. Photograph by Lewis Hines, courtesy of George Eastman House (GEH 43206).

The Edison Lamp Works factory in Newark, New Jersey. Women's Bureau photograph, courtesy of the National Archives at College Park (RG 86G-2H-1).

The year 1919 also brought a bitter split within the ranks of the feminist leaders, who were forced to reexamine the question of protecting women workers. Florence Clark and Helen Ross had begun to wrestle with the problem as they found themselves insisting on women's right to keep their storeroom jobs, while denying them the right to load freight and pull heavy carts. Anna Howard Shaw had argued that women did not need protection from men "or any group of people," and now, with the war over, the reformers confronted the unexpected results of protectionism. Women who had learned to do men's jobs suddenly had to compete with men in the labor market. Printers, typesetters, telegraph operators, and streetcar conductors especially needed to be free from restrictions on night work.[38] Laws designed to protect them from long hours and unhealthy conditions now stood in their way.

In June 1919, Congress finally adopted the woman suffrage amendment. It came too late to serve as the war measure that the president had urged, but it was at least partly a response to women's war work. As soon as the amendment passed, many feminist leaders began to call for the next step: an equal rights amendment. Some of them were middle-class women who valued equality in principle more dearly than equality of work conditions; others were working women who felt confined by laws that limited their hours. Together, the two groups began a campaign that set them against the more traditional social reformers.[39] Mary Van Kleeck and Mary Anderson had always insisted that the *job* should be regulated, not the worker; and yet they could not bring themselves to give up the idea of protective laws.[40] Along with Rose Schneiderman and most of the Women's Trade Union League, they fought against the equal rights amendment. Working women, they argued, were still mostly young, inexperienced, and easily exploited, and so they still needed government protection. An equal rights amendment would endanger all of the minimum wage and maximum hours laws that the two Marys, Rose Schneiderman, and the WTUL had fought so hard to win. The suffrage leader Alice Paul, now an equal rights advocate, became so angry that she stopped speaking to Mary Anderson altogether, in spite of all that Anderson had done and would do to help working women.[41] This conflict would not be settled by their generation, but would last well beyond the next world war.[42]

To most of the women war workers, the controversy over equal rights meant very little as they headed into the 1920s. Life and work beckoned, and women were too busy for philosophy or politics. Many of them married, stopped working, and had children. Such had been their plan all along. In the twenties, as in the teens, fewer than 7 percent of white married women worked for wages.[43] Most of the white women who did continue to work, both married and single, slipped back into their traditional workplaces—the garment shops, textile mills, canneries, and restaurants.

About one-third of black women continued to work after marrying, but married and unmarried alike remained largely in domestic service, commercial laundry work, and a few—very few—industries. Mexican women, whose pres-

The war accelerated the movement of women into office work. Women's Bureau photograph, courtesy of the National Archives at College Park (RG 86G-1S-17).

ence in the States had increased during the war, generally did agricultural work, while Asian women—confined mostly to ethnic neighborhoods in West Coast cities—seldom broke out of sewing and food processing work.

Gradually, during the 1920s, new industries provided some cleaner and safer work for some women. The development of the radio and the increasing electrification of America opened up jobs in modern, well-ordered factories, where women could do the small, delicate work of that era's high-tech industries.

For the younger white women, there were also more and more opportunities in the pink collar world of office work. As new methods and new machinery in offices opened jobs to young women, more girls began to finish high school.[44]

Though they enjoyed higher social status and earned higher pay than the factory workers, and though they increasingly held high school diplomas, female clerks and typists knew that they would never advance along with the office boys. And so, even as work in offices increased, most women still found themselves confined to jobs with no ladder to climb, no training for the future, no chance to make a wage that could really support a family.[45] Then, when they did marry, even those who might have wished to remain at work were often driven from their jobs by company policies that forbade the employment of married women.

By 1930, the teenagers of 1912, the young war workers of 1917, were reaching middle age. Through the Great Depression, even those who wanted to work found that government policy, a shortage of jobs, and intense social pressure made married women quite unwelcome in the workplace. By 1940, as Hitler was overrunning western Europe, the daughters of former munition makers had begun working in America's garment factories, commercial laundries, telephone exchanges, and typing pools.

When the United States entered the Second World War and women were again called upon to keep their county's war machinery going, most Americans thought that Rosie the Riveter and Wendy the Welder were doing something new. As Mary Anderson complained in her autobiography, "No one [in 1942] seemed to know anything about what women had done in World War I."[46] The "making munitions is woman's job" slogan had never really taken hold, because the American part in the war had been so short, the recruiting drive so late. Middle-class women had never fully entered the workforce, and working-class women hadn't needed a long media campaign to persuade them to switch jobs and earn higher wages. For the most part, the women in the munitions plants of the First World War had been seen as workers—workers often resented by the men around them—and not symbols of patriotic service. When the war ended, they were not simply driven away; they were forgotten.

Epilogue: 1945

MILDRED OWEN was a bit old for a welder, but she gave it a try anyway.[1] The women getting all the attention were the young ones who looked pretty in their checkered bandanas and whose goggles didn't accentuate any wrinkles on their faces. Norman Rockwell's Rosie the Riveter had firm muscles in her arms and a little pink powder puff sticking out of her overalls pocket. But Mildred, a forty-something divorced mother of two, was needed along with the athletic young women. American involvement in this war had gone on much longer than the last one—four weary years instead of only nineteen months.

In the First World War, more than a million American women had worked in plants that produced war products, and countless others had taken men's places in the secondary industries that allowed the war machine to keep running. Most of these women, however, had simply shifted from other industries, and most of them had been young and single. Just when nonworking women were about to be mobilized, the armistice was signed.

During World War II, women's wartime labor involved more than a shift of young women from corset factories to cartridge plants. Certainly there was a good bit of transferring from one job to another: white working women again moved into nontraditional and better-paying work. Black, Mexican, Chinese, and Native American women migrated to the cities and the seaports, where for the first time they had easy access to skilled industrial jobs.[2] But there were also

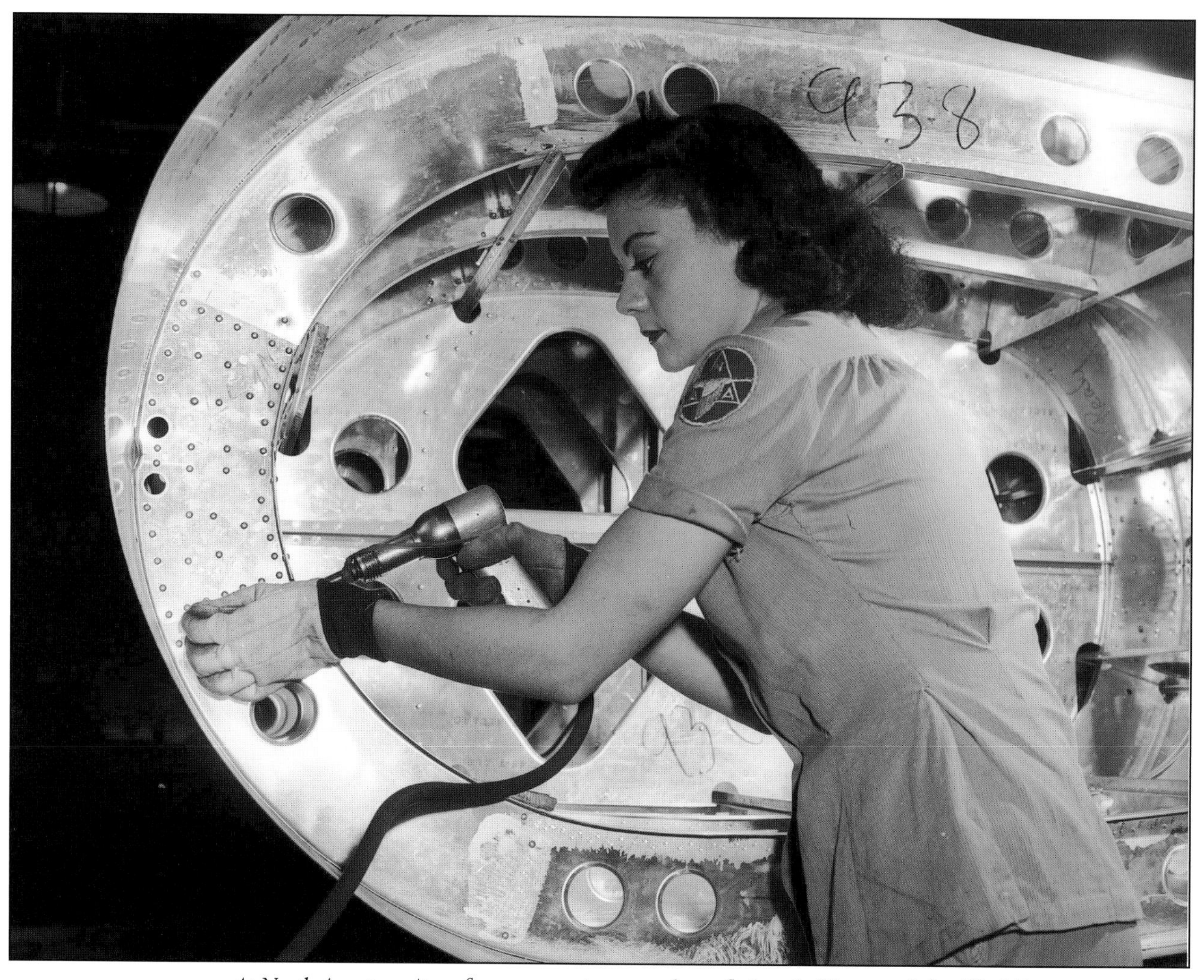

At North American Aircraft, a woman rivets together a fuel tank. Photograph by Alfred T. Palmer for the Office of War Information. Courtesy of the Library of Congress, Prints and Photographs Division, FSA/OWI Collection (LC USW3-055278-C).

many new workers. Middle-class women who had never before held a job became shell inspectors, welders, machinists, riveters. College women went into factories rather than into office or professional work. By the end of the war, 6 million nonworking American women had taken jobs. Among them, in far greater numbers than during World War I, were middle-aged working-class women who went back to work after many years of homemaking and child care.

Mildred Owen was one of these. Born in Boston in 1903, she was the youngest of eleven children of a sheet-metal worker and his homemaker wife. In

1918, the pressure to drop out of school and take a job became too great, and Mildred—at the age of fifteen—went to work at a leather factory, running a machine that pressed out parts for shoes. When the factory inspectors came around, young Mildred would run up to the attic and slip in between the hides that hung down from the ceiling, sometimes waiting there for a couple of hours until the inspectors had left.

She lived at home and turned over her five-dollars-a-week pay envelope to her mother, who gave her fifty cents each week for her own expenses and pleasure. At the factory every day she worked at her leather pressing machine. Shoe heel counters and boxed toes that had been soaked in water and glue curled up as they dried, and Mildred fed them into a big rolling machine to flatten them. Then one day her hand slipped and the machine mashed one finger and cut off the tip of another.

A missing fingertip on the right hand didn't keep one from working when food prices were so high and jobs were so plentiful and the country was at war. Mildred next tried working on the night shift at a gunpowder factory, where at five o'clock one morning she heard an explosion and looked out the window in time to see part of the building blowing up and a man flying out among the debris. She soon left that job, not because of the explosion, but because of her body's reaction to the chemicals. She would later remember being "puffed up" and yellow and "very, very sick." Mildred also had the flu during the epidemic of 1918, but she was one of the strong ones who survived.

Then the war ended, and over the next few years Mildred waited tables, worked in a box factory, and spent some time as a housemaid. She married in 1929—the year of the great stock market crash. Through the Great Depression, Mildred stayed at home to care for her two little boys, getting by on government relief checks because her husband had no work and because often he was not even around.

Then came another war, and Mildred went back to work. In 1943, she finally divorced her husband and set out alone to support herself and her sons. She worked in a shipyard in Massachusetts, did laundry at a military camp in Arizona, and ended up at the North American Aircraft plant in California. In all of these jobs, Mildred preferred the night shift, which started after her sons had gone to bed and ended in time for her to get home and send them off to school. She was now past forty, while most of the other welders were in their early twenties.

Hard as she tried, Mildred could not succeed as a welder. The job required some skill or strength or agility that she could not muster. Soon she dropped down to welder's marker. By the end of the war, she was working as a matron in the women's rest room, keeping the room tidy, making coffee, and selling doughnuts to the younger women who worked on the shop floor. The entire country was mobilized, and Mildred continued to do her part.

Mildred had been, at the age of fifteen, one of the youngest munitions workers of the First World War. Those who were a few years older—twenty or

In North American's plastics department, a woman employee drills a part while it is held firmly on a jig. Photograph by Alfred T. Palmer for the Office of War Information. Courtesy of the Library of Congress, Prints and Photographs Division, FSA/OWI Collection (LC USW3-055161-C).

twenty-two in 1918—were not yet fifty when the Japanese bombed Pearl Harbor. Of the 6 million women who entered, or reentered, the workforce during the Second World War, more than 1.5 million were between the ages of forty-five and sixty-five. Old enough to be the mothers of the young and pink-cheeked Rosies, they nonetheless left their homes and took up work in the war factories alongside the younger women. Another quarter of a million women over the age of sixty-five also entered, or reentered, the workforce during the Second World War.[3] These last, perhaps, should be called Rosie's grandmothers.

These two groups of new and returning older women joined another 3 million women over forty-five who were already in the workforce before World War II began, and who had been working pretty steadily since adolescence.[4] Whether returning to the workforce or continuing but transferring from peacetime jobs, married and older women had a far stronger presence in the war industries of the Second World War. How many of these mature women had actually worked in the war industries of 1918 we will never know, but surely Mildred Owen was not alone.

When women came back into heavy industry and munitions work during World War II, they were more desperately needed, and so they were more graciously received. Government posters and popular songs proclaimed that women were working for more than wages, while movie stars and popular singers visited the factories to encourage and congratulate them. Many of the women worked through all four years of the war, developing high levels of skill in their new jobs, helping the country build prodigious numbers of planes and ships, turning America into "the arsenal of democracy."

At the end of the war, although they were again unceremoniously driven from men's jobs, women's contributions to the war effort persisted in the public memory and remained part of their own self-images.[5] Their ability to do skilled work and earn wages equal to men's would not, this time, be so quickly and thoroughly forgotten. After a flourishing of domesticity in the 1950s—perhaps a welcome relief from the hard years of the Depression and the war—women in the 1960s would finally demand entry into the professions and trades that had been closed to them.[6] The connection between war work in the 1940s and the women's movement of the 1960s is still being debated by historians and economists, but few would argue that any benefits of feminism in the workplace came too late for women already past middle age.

Mildred Owen, with her ninth-grade education and her crippled hand,

Electric arc welders at the Landers, Frary, and Clark plant in New Britain, Connecticut. Photograph by Gordon Parks for the Office of War Information. Courtesy of the Library of Congress, Prints and Photographs Division, FSA/OWI Collection (LC-USW3-034283-C).

spent the 1960s working for low wages at a doughnut shop and a dry cleaner's store. An elderly woman with few options, she still needed to work, just as she had in 1917 when she left school to take a job in a leather factory, and brought her pay envelope home to her mother.

■

Working women of the generation born around the turn of the century earned little praise and few lasting opportunities during the First World War. Still, they had accomplished much. In the midst of a national crisis, more than a million women had moved boldly into war jobs, where they proved their adaptability and their grit. They pushed heavy trucks, mixed chemicals, assembled airplanes, and learned to weld and rivet and operate machine tools. They died in explosions and lost fingers and hands in machinery. They inhaled noxious fumes and faced down prejudice. They struggled to establish their own rights, and they helped win the war.

Although they then left heavy industry, going back to the women's trades or leaving paid work altogether, these women did, in fact, leave a legacy in the workplace. Their courage and willingness to take on war work forced America to consider more carefully their working conditions. The perception—perhaps the illusion—that a munitions factory threatened femininity in ways that a textile mill did not brought pressure to make factories safer and cleaner. The need to attract and keep intelligent working women—and the potential need to attract "wageless" women—also prompted reform. Chairs, rest rooms, cafeterias, training schools, and personnel departments appeared; and when these "welfare measures" increased productivity, managers kept them after the war, for men as well as for women. Perhaps these things were coming anyway, but the war certainly hastened their arrival. The war also launched female reformers, with their peculiar blend of maternalism and feminism, into government agencies where they could agitate for change. Mary Anderson would spend the next twenty-odd years at the Department of Labor, educating and advocating for working women. She was still there pressing for equal pay for women during the Second World War.

In short, while female workers of the First World War gained little that was lasting for themselves, they did smooth the way for the next generation. Each had done her part: Caraola Cram and the other skilled toolmakers; Nellie and the "girls" doing unskilled work at Remington–UMC in Bridgeport and in arsenals around the country; black women in the rail yards and the packing plants; white women in the airplane factories and shipyards; Burton Gaither and the other welders and machinists in railroad repair shops; even fifteen-year-old Mildred Owen, who worked in a gunpowder plant only long enough to get sick and verify the danger of the chemicals. They were all Rosie's Mom.

ACKNOWLEDGMENTS

The true heroines and heroes in a project of this kind are the librarians and archivists who collect, preserve, and provide access to historic materials. When the materials are all more than eighty years old, the names of many of these people are lost, but their anonymity does not diminish appreciation. Among those currently working in the field, I especially want to thank Charlotte Bernini and Mary Hardy of the Howe Library in Hanover, New Hampshire, for working miracles with interlibrary loan. I am also indebted to the staff at the Dartmouth College Library, the National Archives in College Park, the Sophia Smith Collection at Smith College, the Radcliffe Institute at Harvard, the Library of Congress, the Kheel Center at Cornell, the Tamiment Institute Library at New York University, the Chicago Historical Society, the University of Nebraska, and the George Eastman House. Special thanks go to Amanda Page at the Springfield Art and Historical Society in Springfield, Vermont, and to Bob Rodriguez, formerly director of the American Precision Museum in Windsor, Vermont.

I am also greatly indebted to Elizabeth Swayze, my editor at Northeastern University Press, for seeing so clearly what I was trying to accomplish and for helping to drag it out of me. I am grateful to Margaret Higonnet and Joyce Berkman for invaluable suggestions on an early draft of the manuscript.

Without the support and enthusiasm of my family and friends, I may have started, but would never have been able to finish, this project. Among the many I will mention only a few: Marisa Smith and Eric Kraus provided encouragement and expert professional advice. Ginny, Betsy, and Steve helped me find balance between the insistence of life's harsh, untimely intrusions and the inevitability of deadlines. Throughout the entire project, my sons, Gavin and Galen, encouraged and supported me by simply assuming that I could succeed; my husband, Yorke, by understanding how hard it would really be.

A NOTE ON THE ILLUSTRATIONS

The first large group of photographs in the book were taken by Lewis Hine, one of the greatest documentary photographers of the twentieth century. Working for the National Child Labor Committee beginning in 1908, Hine traveled across America taking pictures and interviewing children who worked in factories, mines, and mills; on farms as berry pickers; in seaside sheds shucking oysters; and on city street corners as "newsies" and bootblacks. His photographs, taken with a clear social and political purpose, helped bring about passage of the first federal child labor law in 1916. Hine also, throughout his career, photographed men and women at work. In his early photographs women and children, especially, seem to be burdened by their work. Later in his career, Hine focused more on the satisfactions and nobility of certain kinds of labor.

The second large group of images comes from the records of the Women's Bureau of the Department of Labor. Early in November 1918, just before the war ended, the Woman in Industry Service asked employers around the country to send in photographs showing women at work. In response, the service received several hundred photographs, which were then used for posters and slide shows to illustrate good and bad working conditions.[1] On the backs of most of the photographs, the Woman in Industry Service staff wrote captions identifying the task or the company. Some of the captions also include evaluative comments such as "good lighting" or "no seats provided."

The War Department and the Signal Corps also collected photographs during the First World War. Both agencies made some effort to record not just the soldiers but also the workers in war industries.

During the Second World War, the Office of Emergency Management hired professional photographers to document the war on the home front. Alfred T. Palmer created thousands of images, which were then published in magazines, newspapers, and books. Gordon Parks, working for the Farm Security Administration, produced photographs of both rural and urban America. Many of the photographs by Palmer and Parks are clearly meant to inspire and celebrate, as well as to record the war effort.

The two posters included in *Rosie's Mom* were created through the Division of Pictorial Publicity, a group of artists headed by Charles Dana Gibson. Gibson had been recruited by George Creel, head of the Committee on Public Information, to help publicize the government's war aims and to build support for the war effort. Donating their work to the cause, the artists of the Division of Pictorial Publicity submitted seven hundred poster designs and hundreds of other images to government departments and patriotic committees.[2] The drawing for the newspaper advertisement in Chapter 6 was almost certainly produced by one of the artists in Gibson's group.

The remaining illustrations in *Rosie's Mom* come from a variety of sources. Unfortunately, most of the photographers are unknown and we can only guess at the feelings and motivations of those who created the images. All of them, however, give us a sense that the women pictured were doing something remarkable.

NOTES

Abbreviations

BWEGM James Grossman, ed., *Black Workers in the Era of the Great Migration* (University Publications of America, 1985). 25 reels of microfilm.

MVK Mary van Kleeck Collection, Sophia Smith Archive, Smith College.

NACP National Archives at College Park, Maryland.

PWTUL Papers of the Women's Trade Union League, microfilm collection (Research Publications, 1981). 131 reels. For a guide to these papers, see Edward T. James, ed., *Papers of the Women's Trade Union League and Its Principal Leaders: Guide to the Microfilm Edition* (Woodbridge, Conn.: Research Publications, 1981).

WSS Women's Service Section, United States Railroad Administration

Chapter 1

1. Amy Hewes, *Women as Munition Makers: A Study of Conditions in Bridgeport, Connecticut* (New York: Russell Sage Foundation, 1917).
2. Robert H. Ferrell, *Woodrow Wilson and World War I, 1917–1921* (New York: Harper & Row, 1985), 4.
3. Judy Yung, *Unbound Feet: A Social History of Chinese Women in San Francisco* (Berkeley: University of California Press, 1995), 135.
4. From a statement made by Pauline Newman, cited in Nancy Schrom Dye, *As Equals and as Sisters: Feminism, Unionism, and the Women's Trade Union League of New York* (Columbia: University of Missouri Press, 1980), 143.
5. According to the Bureau of Labor Statistics, reported in Basil Manly and Francis Patrick Walsh, *Final Report of the Commission on Industrial Relations* (Chicago: Barnard and Miller, 1915), 10.
6. Josephine Goldmark, "Working Women and the Laws: A Record of Neglect," National Consumer's League, reprinted from *The Annals of the American Academy of Political and Social Science* 28, no. 2 (1906): 261, MVK, box 71, folder 111.
7. Elizabeth Dole and Jean M. Curtis, "A Message from the Secretary of Labor," *Milestones: The Women's Bureau Celebrates 70 Years of Women's Labor History,* 1990, <http://www.inform.umd.edu/EdRes/Topic/Womens Studies/GenderIssues/WomenInWorkforce/womens-labor-history> (26 October 2001).

8. Elizabeth Beardsley Butler, *Women and the Trades: Pittsburgh, 1907–1908* (New York: Charities Publication Committee, 1909; reprint, Pittsburgh: University of Pittsburgh Press, 1984), 25, 37.
9. Leslie Woodcock Tentler, *Wage-Earning Women: Industrial Work and Family Life in the United States, 1900–1930* (New York: Oxford University Press, 1979), 30–31.
10. Mary Van Kleeck, "The Millinery Trade and the Problems Which It Illustrates," MVK, box 96, folder 1504; Tentler, *Wage-Earning Women,* 31.
11. Butler, *Pittsburgh,* 33.
12. Louise C. Odencrantz, *Italian Women in Industry: A Study of Conditions in New York City* (New York: Russell Sage Foundation, 1919),108–9.
13. William J. Breen, *Labor Market Politics and the Great War: The Department of Labor, the States, and the First U.S. Employment Service, 1907–1933* (Kent, Ohio: Kent State University Press, 1997), 3.
14. Odencrantz, *Italian Women,* 118.
15. Elizabeth Hasanovitz, *One of Them: Chapters from a Passionate Autobiography* (Boston: Houghton Mifflin, 1918), 92.
16. Robert Wagner (chairman of the New York State Factory Investigating Commission), "The Factory Inquiry," *New York Times,* 10 March 1913, 8.
17. William L. O'Neill, *Everyone Was Brave: The Rise and Fall of Feminism in America* (Chicago: Quadrangle, 1969), 151.
18. Jane Addams, *The Spirit of Youth and the City Streets* (New York: Macmillan, 1909), 5.
19. Yung, *Unbound Feet,* 94.
20. Mary Van Kleeck, "Some Problems of Method in Investigation of Women's Work," typed article, c. 1908, MVK, box 100, folder 1563. Late in her life, Mary Van Kleeck discovered that her ancestors had spelled the name van Kleeck with the lower-case v, and she began to use the older spelling. I have retained the upper-case V, which appears in all of her early publications and in her signature on documents from the period of the First World War.
21. *Muller v. the State of Oregon,* 1908, quoted in U.S. Department of Labor, Women's Bureau, bulletin no. 14. See also Maurine Greenwald, Introduction to Butler, *Pittsburgh,* xxix.
22. Margaret Dreier Robins, "Proceedings of the Third Biennial Convention of the National Women's Trade Union League," 1911; quoted in Dye, *As Equals,* 11–12.
23. Dorothy Schneider and Carl J. Schneider, *Into the Breach: American Women Overseas during World War I* (New York: Viking, 1991), chapter 1.

Chapter 2

1. "Strong men sat with tears rolling down their faces. Her pathos and earnestness held audiences spellbound" (M. Sherwood to Harriet Taylor Upton, 15 July 1912, PWTUL, Rose Schneiderman Papers, reel 1).

2. Annelise Orleck, *Common Sense and a Little Fire: Women and Working-Class Politics in the United States, 1900–1965* (Chapel Hill: University of North Carolina Press, 1995), 10.
3. Ibid., 17.
4. Rose Schneiderman, *All for One* (New York: P. S. Eriksson, 1967), 49.
5. Ibid., 62.
6. Review of *A Seasonal Industry: A Study of the Millinery Trade* by Mary Van Kleeck, *New Republic* 12 (1917): 55–56.
7. Dye, *As Equals,* 25.
8. Schneiderman, *All for One,* 50; see also Theresa Serber Malkiel, *Diary of a Shirtwaist Striker* (New York: Co-operative Press, 1910; reprint, Ithaca: ILR Press, 1990).
9. Martha Bensley Bruere, "The White Goods Strikers," *Life and Labor* 3 (March 1913): 73–75.
10. Schneiderman, *All for One,* 84–86.
11. Ibid., 86–87.
12. Orleck, *Common Sense,* 88.
13. Mary Van Kleeck, "Lecture I," MVK, box 96, folder 1504.
14. *New York Times,* 14 December 1909; quoted in Philip S. Foner, *Women and the American Labor Movement: From Colonial Times to the Eve of World War I* (New York: Free Press, 1979).
15. Foner, *Women and the American Labor Movement: From Colonial Times,* 332; Dye, *As Equals,* 91–93, 126.
16. Schneiderman, *All for One,* 90.
17. Ibid., 94–95.
18. Foner, *Women and the American Labor Movement: From Colonial Times,* 335–38.
19. *New York Times,* 27 November 1910.
20. *New York Times,* 26 March 1911.
21. Eyewitness report by William G. Shepherd, *Milwaukee Journal,* 27 March 1911; quoted in Leon Stein, ed., *Out of the Sweatshop: The Struggle for Industrial Democracy* (New York: Quandrangle/The New York Times Book Co., 1977), 193.
22. Schneiderman, *All for One,* 98–99.
23. As reported in the *New York Times;* quoted in Schneiderman, *All for One,* 100–101.
24. Dye, *As Equals,* 145.
25. Mary Van Kleeck to John M. Glenn, 12 November 1912, MVK, box 100, folder 1564; Odencrantz, *Italian Women,* 89–91; Susan Lehrer, *Origins of Protective Legislation for Women, 1905–1925* (Albany: State University of New York Press, 1987), 159.
26. Orleck, *Common Sense,* 22–23, 38.

27. Bruere, "The White Goods Strikers," 73.
28. Rose Schneiderman, "The White Goods Workers of New York: Their Struggle for Human Conditions," *Life and Labor* 3 (1913): 136.
29. *New York Times,* 29 January 1913, 30 January 1913.
30. *New York Times,* 31 January 1913.
31. *New York Times,* 16 January 1913, 3; 26 January 1913.
32. Foner, *Women and the American Labor Movement: From Colonial Times,* 371.
33. Schneiderman, "The White Goods Workers of New York," 136.
34. Foner, *Women and the American Labor Movement: From Colonial Times,* 372.
35. *New York Times,* 22 January 1913, 1.
36. Schneiderman, "The White Goods Workers of New York." See also Schneiderman, *All for One,* 104–9.
37. Manly and Walsh, *Final Report of the Commission,* 71–73.
38. Graham Adams, *The Age of Industrial Violence, 1910–1915: The Activities and Findings of the U.S. Commission on Industrial Relations* (New York: Columbia University Press, 1966), 73–74.
39. *The Call,* 12 January 1914; quoted in Philip S. Foner, *The Industrial Workers of the World, 1905–1917,* vol. 4 of *History of the Labor Movement in the United States* (New York: International Publishers, 1975), 436.
40. *New York Times,* 12 February 1914; cited in Foner, *The Industrial Workers,* 442.
41. Elizabeth Gurley Flynn, *The Rebel Girl: The Autobiography of My First Life, 1906–1926* (1955; reprint, New York: International Publishers, 1973), 188.
42. Orleck, *Common Sense,* 107; Dye, *As Equals,* 134.
43. Hasanovitz, *One of Them,* 280.
44. Foner, *The Industrial Workers,* 451–52.

Chapter 3

1. See, for example, *New York Times,* 11 July 1915, 9.
2. See, for example, the *Bridgeport Evening Post,* 18 January 1916, 19.
3. Description from Butler, *Pittsburgh,* 102.
4. Odencrantz, *Italian Women,* 47.
5. Butler, *Pittsburgh,* 258.
6. *New York Times,* 19 July 1915, 4.
7. Hewes, *Women as Munition Makers,* 15.
8. *Bridgeport Evening Post,* 31 January 1916.
9. *New York Times,* 19 July 1915, 4.
10. Hewes, *Women as Munition Makers,* 15.
11. *New York Times,* 24 and 25 July 1915.
12. *Bridgeport Evening Post,* 4 January 1916.
13. *New York Times,* 14 July 1915, 1.
14. *New York Times,* 15 July 1915, 3.

15. James J. Kenneally, *Women and the American Trade Unions* (St. Albans, Vt.: Eden Press, 1978), 87; *New York Times,* 18 July 1915, 2.
16. *New York Times,* 20 July 1915, 4.
17. *New York Times,* 21 July 1915, 1.
18. *New York Times,* 22 and 23 July 1915.
19. *New York Times,* 24 July 1915, 1.
20. Philip S. Foner, *On the Eve of America's Entrance into World War I, 1915–1916,* vol. 6 of *History of the Labor Movement in the United States* (New York: International Publishers, 1975), 195–96.
21. Reprinted ibid., 196.
22. *Bridgeport Evening Post,* 18 January 1916, 19.
23. *Bridgeport Evening Post,* 9 April 1916.
24. Madeleine P. Grant, "In Memoriam—Amy Hewes," Hewes Collection, Mount Holyoke College Archives.
25. Hewes, *Women as Munition Makers,* 19–20.
26. Ibid., 77–78.
27. Ibid., 29–30.
28. Ibid., 44.
29. Ibid., 36.
30. Hewes, "Women as Munition Makers," *The Survey* 37, no. 14 (January 6, 1917): 383.
31. Hewes, *Women as Munition Makers,* 33–36.
32. *Bridgeport Post,* 19 February 1916, 9.
33. *Bridgeport Post,* 21 March 1916.
34. Ruth Ogden, "Health Inspector's Life Is Not a Merry One," *Bridgeport Sunday Post,* 6 February 1916, 13.
35. Hewes, *Women as Munition Makers,* 79, and Hewes, "Women as Munition Makers," 383–84.
36. Ruth Ogden, "City Faces Problem in Housing Thousands of Girls Who Flock Here in Search of Work," *Bridgeport Sunday Post,* 6 February 1916, 13, 22.
37. *Bridgeport Post,* 22 April 1916, 14.
38. Ogden, "City Faces Problem," 13, 22.
39. Hewes, *Women as Munition Makers,* 83–84; *Bridgeport Sunday Post,* 30 January 1916.
40. *Bridgeport Post,* 11 February 1916.
41. Hewes, *Women as Munition Makers,* 79–80.
42. Ibid., 65–67.
43. Ibid., 93.
44. Ibid., 47.
45. Ibid.
46. Hewes, "Women as Munition Makers," 380–81.
47. Hewes, *Women as Munition Makers,* 60.

48. Ibid., 7–8.
49. Edward Robb Ellis, *Echoes of Distant Thunder: Life in the United States, 1914–1918* (New York: Coward, McCann & Geoghegan, 1975), 191–92.
50. "Retail Prices of Food in the United States," *Monthly Labor Review* 3 (1916): 322–24.
51. *New York Times,* 18 and 20 February 1916.
52. *New York Times,* 21 April 1916, 8.
53. *New York Times,* 23 April 1916, 5.
54. Foner, *On the Eve,* 196–99.
55. *New York Times,* 23 April 1916, 5.
56. Manly and Walsh, *Final Report of the Commission,* 3.
57. Valerie Jean Conner, *The National War Labor Board: Stability, Social Justice, and the Voluntary State in World War I* (Chapel Hill: University of North Carolina Press, 1983), 16.

Chapter 4

1. Emmett J. Scott, ed., "Additional Letters of Negro Migrants of 1916–1918," *Journal of Negro History* 4 (1919): 457–58.
2. *Defender,* 10 February 1917.
3. Emmett J. Scott, *Negro Migration during the War,* no. 16 of *Preliminary Economic Studies of the War,* ed. David Kinley (New York: Oxford University Press, 1920), 49, 52.
4. All together, the railroads brought about twelve thousand men north in the period around the First World War. See Scott, *Negro Migration during the War,* 54–55; Joe W. Trotter and Earl Lewis, eds., *African Americans in the Industrial Age: A Documentary History, 1915–1945* (Boston: Northeastern University Press, 1996), 26–32.
5. Chicago Commission on Race Relations, *The Negro in Chicago: A Study of Race Relations and a Race Riot* (Chicago: University of Chicago Press, 1922), 386.
6. Scott, "Additional Letters," 419, 422.
7. Jacqueline Jones, *Labor of Love, Labor of Sorrow: Black Women, Work, and the Family from Slavery to the Present* (New York: Basic Books, 1985; reprint, New York: Vintage Books, 1986), 113; William H. Harris, *The Harder We Run: Black Workers Since the Civil War* (New York: Oxford University Press, 1982), 23–24; see also Claudia Goldin, *Understanding the Gender Gap: An Economic History of Women* (New York: Oxford University Press, 1990).
8. Jones, *Labor of Love,* 137; U.S. Department of Labor, Women's Bureau, "Negro Women in Industry," bulletin no. 20, 1922, 37–38.
9. Jones, *Labor of Love,* 132–33.
10. Trotter and Lewis, *African Americans in the Industrial Age,* 42–47.
11. W. H. Harris, *The Harder We Run,* 30–31.

12. Foner, *On the Eve,* 210.
13. *Defender,* 3 February 1917, 1.
14. Emmett J. Scott, "Letters of Negro Migrants of 1916–1918," *Journal of Negro History* 4 (1919): 318.
15. Scott, *Negro Migration during the War,* 30.
16. James R. Grossman, *Land of Hope: Chicago, Black Southerners, and the Great Migration* (Chicago: University of Chicago Press, 1989), 79.
17. Chicago Commission on Race Relations, *The Negro in Chicago,* 87.
18. Scott, "Additional Letters," 417.
19. Scott, *Negro Migration during the War,* 72.
20. *Defender,* 24 March 1917, 1.
21. Maurine Greenwald, *Women, War, and Work: The Impact of World War I on Women Workers in the United States* (Westport, Conn.: Greenwood Press, 1980), 113.
22. Scott, *Negro Migration during the War,* 135.
23. *Defender,* 24 February 1917.
24. Scott, "Letters of Negro Migrants," 317.
25. Ibid.
26. Ibid., 316.
27. James Grossman, *Land of Hope,* 103–5.
28. Chicago Commission on Race Relations, *The Negro in Chicago,* 79; Scott, *Negro Migration during the War,* 54–58, 102.
29. Langston Hughes, *The Big Sea* (New York: Alfred A. Knopf, 1945), 33.
30. "The Phyllis Wheatley Home for Girls," c. 1966, pamphlet in Phyllis Wheatley Home Records, Special Collections, University of Illinois at Chicago; Joanne J. Meyerowitz, *Women Adrift: Independent Wage Earners in Chicago, 1880–1930* (Chicago: University of Chicago Press, 1988), 54.
31. Anne Meis Knupfer, *Toward a Tenderer Humanity and a Nobler Womanhood: African American Women's Clubs in Turn-of-the-Century Chicago* (New York: New York University Press, 1996), 84.
32. Anne Meis Knupfer, "'If You Can't Push, Pull, If You Can't Pull, Please Get Out of the Way': The Phyllis Wheatley Club and Home in Chicago, 1896 to 1920," *Journal of Negro History* 82 (1997): 227.
33. Alice Dunbar-Nelson, "Negro Women in War Work," in *Scott's Official History of the American Negro in the World War,* ed. Emmett Scott (1919; reprint, New York: Arno Press, 1969), 393–94.
34. Arvarh E. Strickland, *History of the Chicago Urban League* (Urbana: University of Illinois Press, 1966), 29–30.
35. "First Annual Report of the Chicago League on Urban Conditions among Negroes, For the Fiscal Year Ended October 31st, 1917," University of Illinois at Chicago.
36. Chicago Commission on Race Relations, *The Negro in Chicago,* 95–96.

37. See Jacqueline Jones, *Labor of Love,* 99–100, on blacks' participation "in a rural folk culture based upon group cooperation rather than male competition and the accumulation of goods."
38. For a description of early-twentieth-century commercial laundries, see Butler, *Pittsburgh,* chapters 9–11.
39. Chicago Commission on Race Relations, *The Negro in Chicago,* 95–96.
40. See Agnes Nestor's account in her *Woman's Labor Leader* (Rockford, Ill.: Bellevue Books, 1954).
41. Allan H. Spear, *Black Chicago: The Making of a Negro Ghetto, 1890–1920* (Chicago: University of Chicago Press, 1967), 164; Chicago Commission on Race Rela-tions, *The Negro in Chicago,* 414–15.
42. Scott, "Additional Letters," 435.
43. Rick Halpern, *Down on the Killing Floor* (Chicago: University of Illinois Press, 1997), 47.
44. Ibid., 45–56; U.S. Department of Labor, Women's Bureau, "Negro Women in Industry in 15 States," bulletin no. 70 (Washington, D.C.:1929), 18–19.
45. W. H. Harris, *The Harder We Run,* 55; Jacqueline Jones, *Labor of Love,* 166.
46. Alma Herbst, *The Negro in the Slaughtering and Meat-Packing Industry in Chicago* (Boston: Houghton Mifflin, 1932), 170–71.
47. Transcript of Alschuler hearings, BWEGM, reel 2.
48. Halpern, *Down on the Killing Floor,* 54.
49. Ibid., 58–60.
50. Elizabeth Lindsay Davis, *The Story of the Illinois Federation of Women's Clubs* (1921; reprint, New York: G. K. Hall, 1997), 67; Elizabeth Lindsay Davis, *Lifting as They Climb* (1933; reprint, New York: G. K. Hall, 1996), 142.
51. Elizabeth Anne Payne, *Reform, Labor, and Feminism: Margaret Dreier Robins and the Women's Trade Union League* (Chicago: University of Illinois Press, 1988), 53–54.
52. Halpern, *Down on the Killing Floor,* 52.
53. From the Mary McDowell Papers, quoted in *The Black Worker from 1900 to 1919,* vol. 5 of *Black Workers: A Documentary History from Colonial Times to the Present,* ed. Philip S. Foner and Ronald L. Lewis (Philadelphia: Temple University Press, 1980), 301.
54. See Halpern, *Down on the Killing Floor,* chapter 2; James R. Barrett, *Work and Community in the Jungle: Chicago's Packinghouse Workers, 1894–1922* (Chicago: University of Chicago Press: 1987), 197; Spear, *Black Chicago,* 159; Chicago Commission on Race Relations, *The Negro in Chicago,* 427; Olive M. Sullivan, "The Women's Part in the Stockyards Organization Work," *Life and Labor* 7 (May 1918): 102, 104.
55. Judge Alschuler, quoted in the *Washington Post,* 31 March 1918, 17.
56. Ida Glatt, quoted in Halpern, *Down on the Killing Floor,* 54–55; Mary Anderson, *Woman at Work: The Autobiography of Mary Anderson as Told to Mary N. Winslow*

(Minneapolis: University of Minnesota Press, 1951), 69–70.

57. Ida Glatt to Agnes Nestor, 22 April 1918, PWTUL, Agnes Nestor Papers, reel 2.
58. Women's Bureau, bulletin no. 20, 35.
59. "Colored Women as Industrial Workers in Philadelphia: A Study Made by the Consumers' League of Eastern Pennsylvania," 1920, 10, Division of Archives and Manuscripts, Commonwealth of Pennsylvania.
60. Chicago Commission on Race Relations, *The Negro in Chicago,* 383–84.
61. Ibid., 99.
62. On Detroit, see Women's Bureau, bulletin no. 20, 7–8; Scott, *Negro Migration during the War,* 129–31; Richard W. Thomas, *Life for Us Is What We Make It: Building Black Community in Detroit, 1915–1945* (Bloomington: Indiana University Press, 1992), 32–33.
63. Forrester B. Washington, "Reconstruction and the Colored Woman," *Life and Labor* 9 (1919): 5.
64. "Eureka Thrift Association" in Robb, ed., *The Negro in Chicago, 1779 to 1929,* in *The Wonder Book* series (Chicago: Washington Intercollegiate Club of Chicago, 1929), 143.
65. Women's Bureau, bulletin no. 20, 28.
66. Ibid., 46.
67. See, for example, *Defender,* 6 October 1917, 7.
68. Scott, "Additional Letters," 464, 457, 465.

Chapter 5

1. Mary V. Robinson, "Mary Anderson," typescript, June 1944, PWTUL, Mary Anderson Papers, reel 4.
2. Mary Anderson, *Woman at Work,* 84; Agnes Nestor, *Woman's Labor Leader,* 172–73; David M. Kennedy, *Over Here: The First World War and American Society* (New York: Oxford University Press, 1980), 286.
3. Mary Anderson, *Woman at Work,* chapters 1, 2, and 3.
4. Ibid., 22.
5. Ibid., 44–47; Edward J. James, ed., *Papers of the Women's Trade Union League and Its Principal Leaders: Guide to the Microfilm Edition* (Woodbridge, Conn.: Research Publications, 1981),162.
6. Mary Anderson to Agnes Nestor, 18 January 1918, PWTUL, Agnes Nestor Papers, reel 2.
7. Ida Clyde Clarke, *American Women and the World War* (New York: D. Appleton and Company, 1918).
8. Mary Anderson, *Woman at Work,* 84–85.
9. Eleanor Flexner and Ellen Fitzpatrick, *Century of Struggle: The Woman's Rights Movement in the United States* (Cambridge, Mass.: The Belknap Press of Harvard University Press, 1996), 278.

10. Mary Anderson, *Woman at Work,* 86.
11. Guy Alchon, "Mary Van Kleeck and Social-Economic Planning," *Journal of Policy History* 3 (1991): 1–23.
12. See *New York Times,* 10 July 1917; Scott, *Scott's Official History,* Appendix E.
13. Leonard P. Ayres to Mary Van Kleeck, 30 July 1917, MVK, box 10, folder 139.
14. MVK, box 72, folder 1128.
15. Mary Van Kleeck, "Storage Bulletin no. 9," 11, MVK, box 72, folder 1125.
16. New York State Committee on Women in Industry, Council of National Defense, "Home-Work on Naval Garments, Brooklyn Navy Yard, N.Y.," typed report, 22 November 1917, Sophonisba Breckinridge Papers, Library of Congress.
17. Mary LaDame, Mayor's Committee of Women on National Defense, "Report on the Inspection of Factories Making Army and Navy Uniforms," 31 August 1917, MVK, box 96, folder 1498. Also in Breckinridge Papers.
18. Ibid.
19. "Uniforms to Be Taken Out of Sweatshops," *Life and Labor* 6 (1917): 158.
20. "Report on an Investigation of the Possible Employment of Women in Government Storage Warehouses in and around Norfolk, Virginia," October 1917, MVK, box 72, folder 1128.
21. Ibid.
22. Ibid.
23. Mary Van Kleeck, "Storage Bulletin no. 9," 19.
24. Committee on Women in Industry, typed draft of bulletin no. 1, RG 86, MLR entry 1, box 1, NACP.
25. Eileen Boris, "Tenement Homework on Army Uniforms: The Gendering of Industrial Democracy during World War I," *Labor History* 32 (1991): 231–52.
26. Joseph P. Lash, "Biographical Essay," in *From the Diaries of Felix Frankfurter: With a Biographical Essay and Notes* (New York: Norton, 1975), 18.
27. Foner, *Labor and World War I, 1914–1918,* vol. 7 of *History of the Labor Movement in the United States,* 179; Michael E. Parrish, *Felix Frankfurter and His Times: The Reform Years* (New York: Free Press, 1982), 84; Lash, "Biographical Essay," 18.
28. Minutes of the Women in Industry Advisory Committee, 3 December 1917, PWTUL, Agnes Nestor Papers, reel 1.
29. Kennedy, *Over Here,* 262; and Foner, *Labor and World War I,* 169.
30. Mary Anderson, *Woman at Work,* 86–87.
31. Mary Van Kleeck, "Women in the Munitions Industries," *Life and Labor* 8 (1918): 115–22.
32. See printed report from Amy Hewes to Clara Tead, 23 April 1918–13 December 1918, RG 86, MLR entry 1, box 1, NACP.
33. "Memorandum Regarding Work Done during the War by Miss Mary Van

Kleeck," RG 86, MLR entry 1, box 1, NACP; also Heidi Marshall at Mount Holyoke College library, personal e-mail (24 July 2000).

34. Mary Anderson, *Woman at Work,* 90.
35. Mary Anderson to Agnes Nestor, 18 January 1918, PWTUL, Agnes Nestor Papers, reel 2.
36. Agnes Nestor to Mary Anderson, 20 January 1918, PWTUL, Agnes Nestor Papers, reel 2.
37. O'Neill, *Everyone Was Brave,* 220–21.
38. Parrish, *Felix Frankfurter,* 51–52.
39. Mary Anderson, *Woman at Work,* 90.
40. Ibid., 90–91.
41. Mary Van Kleeck, "Trade Union Women," *New Republic,* 16 November1918, 74.
42. Mary Anderson, *Woman at Work,* 102–3.
43. Woman in Industry Service study of women in government service, RG 86, MLR entry 1, box 2, NACP.
44. Dorothy Sterling, *Black Foremothers: Three Lives* (New York: Feminist Press, 1988), 144–45; Foner, *Labor and World War I,* 142; "Minutes of Advisory Commission," 3 December 1917, PWTUL, Agnes Nestor Papers, reel 1. Separate lunchrooms, toilets, and locker rooms were also established for the nonwhite women at the government arsenals.
45. Mary Anderson, *Woman at Work,* 108.
46. Mary Van Kleeck, "New Standards for Negro Women in Industry," *Life and Labor* 9 (1919): 134–35.
47. Kennedy, *Over Here,* 169.
48. Meirion Harries and Susie Harries, *The Last Days of Innocence: America at War, 1917–1918* (New York: Random House, 1997), 277.
49. National Industrial Conference Board, "Wartime Employment of Women in the Metal Trades," Research Report no. 8 (Boston, 1918), 69.
50. Orleck, *Common Sense,* 138; Schneiderman, *All for One,* 128.
51. Women's Bureau, "Standards for Employment of Women in Industry," bulletin no. 3 (December 1918; reprint, Washington, D.C.: GPO, 1921); see also Mary Anderson, *Woman at Work,* 98.
52. U.S. Department of Labor, Women's Bureau, "Health Problems of Women in Industry," bulletin no. 18, 5.
53. Anthony Livesy, *The Historical Atlas of World War I* (New York: Henry Holt, 1994), 159.
54 Ibid., 160–61.
55. Committee on Hazardous Occupations, Minutes from 24 July 1918, RG 86, MLR entry 1, box 1, NACP.
56. U.S. Department of Labor, Women's Bureau bulletin no. 1, reprinted as

"Proposed Employment of Women during the War in the Industries of Niagara Falls, N.Y.," *Monthly Labor Review* 8 (1919): 231–46; see also shortened version published in *Life and Labor* 9 (1919): 21–24, 43–46.

57. "Proposed Employment of Women in the Industries of Niagara Falls," 231–32.
58. Mary Anderson, *Woman at Work,* 95.
59. "Niagara Falls," typed report, RG 86, MLR entry 8, box 1, NACP.
60. "Proposed Employment of Women in the Industries of Niagara Falls," 243.
61. Ibid., 234.
62. Ibid., 238.
63. Mary Van Kleeck, "The National Importance of Woman's Work," Newsletter of the Woman's Committee, Council of National Defense, 15 September 1918, 1, copy in RG 86, MLR entry 1, box 1, NACP.
64. Ray S. Baker and William E. Dodds, eds., *The Public Papers of Woodrow Wilson,* vol. 5 (New York: Harper & Brothers, 1925–27), 266.

Chapter 6

1. Ruth M. Russell, "For Whom the War Is Not Over," *Life and Labor* 8 (1918): 266–68.
2. On the work or fight order, see Kennedy, *Over Here,* 269; *New Republic,* 1 March 1919, 144–46; John R. Shillady to Woodrow Wilson, 25 September 1918, BWEGM, reel 14.
3. See Maurine Greenwald, *Women, War, and Work,* 116–18; on speed of women in machine shops, see V. B. Turner, "Women in the Mechanical Trades," *Monthly Labor Review* 7 (1918): 687–88, and National Industrial Conference Board, "Wartime Employment of Women."
4. Foner, *Labor and World War I,* 131.
5. "Summary of Certain Plant Investigations," RG 86, MLR entry 7, box 2; NACP.
6. Foner, *Labor and World War I,* 131.
7. U.S. Department of Labor, Women's Bureau, "The New Position of Women in Industry," bulletin no. 12, 33–34.
8. Clara Tead memo, report for the week ending 2 October 1918, RG 86, MLR entry 7, box 2, NACP.
9. Kennedy, *Over Here,* 301.
10. Women's Bureau bulletin no. 12, 106.
11. Anthony Livesey, *The Historical Atlas,* 166.
12. J. V. Hunter, "Service for Women in the Gisholt Shops," *American Machinist* 50 (1919): 8.
13. Peter F. O'Shea, "A Shop Training School for Girls," *Industrial Management* 58 (1919): 213.
14. Women's Bureau bulletin no. 12, 56.

15. Charles U. Carpenter, "How We Trained 5,000 Women," *Industrial Management* 55 (1918): 354.
16. Ibid., 356.
17. Ibid., 357.
18. A report of the National Industrial Conference Board also describes less hostility in shops where women workers were relatives or acquaintances of the men ("Wartime Employment of Women in the Metal Trades," Research Report no. 9, Boston, 1918, 54). On the ease of adapting to machine work among women whose fathers and brothers were machinists, see Turner, "Women in the Mechanical Trades," 687.
19. *Springfield Reporter,* 8 October 1917, 2.
20. *Springfield Reporter,* 21 November 1918, 7.
21. See, for example, James Hartness, *The Human Factor in Works Management* (New York: McGraw-Hill, 1912).
22. "Jones & Lamson Co. to Employ Women," *Springfield Reporter,* 13 December 1917, 1.
23. "Paymaster's report week ending April 5, 1918," typed note in Jones and Lamson historical files, courtesy of Fay Kingsbury and the American Precision Museum.
24. "Jones & Lamson News," *Springfield Reporter,* 12 December 1918.
25. *Springfield Reporter,* 13 December 1917, 1; "Jones & Lamson News," *Springfield Reporter,* 12 December 1918.
26. *Springfield Reporter,* 26 September 1918.
27. *Springfield Reporter,* 3 October 1918.
28. *Springfield Reporter,* 17 October 1918.
29. Amy Hewes to Clara Tead, 23 April 1918–13 December 1918, 47, RG 86, MLR entry 1, box 1, NACP.
30. National Industrial Conference Board, "Wartime Employment of Women," 34.
31. *Springfield Reporter,* 24 October 1918.
32. *New York Times,* 18 September 1918, 10.
33. Fred H. Colvin, "Women in the Machine Shops," *American Machinist* 47 (1917): 509.
34. Joe Christy, *American Aviation: An Illustrated History* (Blue Ridge Summit, Penn.: TAB Books, 1987), 41–42.
35. Women's Bureau bulletin no. 12, 74; Committee on Women in Industry of the Advisory Commission of the Council of National Defense, "Substitution of Women in Aircraft Production," Women in War Industries Series, no. 5, October 1918, RG 86, NACP.
36. See also "Dope Poisoning," *Monthly Labor Review* 3 (1916): 649.
37. Turner, "Women in the Mechanical Trades," 686.
38. Chicago Urban League, "Annual Report for the Fiscal Year Ended October 31,

1919," University of Illinois at Chicago, Department of Special Collections; Chicago Commission on Race Relations, *The Negro in Chicago,* 380–81.

39. Women's Bureau bulletin no. 20, 7–8.
40. Mrs. George Hayes, "Efficiency Plus Spirit of Service," RG 86, MLR entry 1, box 1, NACP.
41. National Industrial Conference Board, "Wartime Employment of Women."
42. *Bridgeport Sunday Post,* 22 September 1918, 1.
43. In an age before television and radio, the wartime Committee on Public Information, headed by George Creel, depended heavily upon a network of local volunteer speakers—the Four Minute Men—who delivered short patriotic addresses in movie theaters and town halls and anywhere else that Americans gathered and could receive messages from the government. A related group, the Four Minute Women, served in less public ways, as was appropriate to middle- and upper-class women at the time. In Bridgeport, after the Four Minute Women began their door-to-door campaign, the local paper began to call them simply the Minute Women.
44. *Bridgeport Sunday Post,* 22 September 1918, 32.
45. Ibid., 36.
46. Conner, *The National War Labor Board,* 104, 130; Bridgeport was producing 7 million rounds of ammunition each week, and was responsible for two-thirds of all ammunition produced in the United States. See Lennie Grimaldi, *Only in Bridgeport: An Illustrated History of the Park City* (1986; reprint, Bridgeport, Conn.: Harbor Publishing, 1993).
47. "Women and the War Labor Board," c. 1919, MVK, box 72, folder 1134.
48. Mary Van Kleeck to Major Tully, Office of the Secretary of War, 25 September 1918, RG 86, MLR entry 1, box 2, NACP.
49. National War Labor Board, *National War Labor Board Docket: A Compilation of the Actions of the National War Labor Board, 1918–1919,* Docket 132, vol. 1 (Washington, D.C., 1919), 5–6; *Bridgeport Evening Post,* 30 August 1910.
50. National War Labor Board, Docket 132.
51. *Bridgeport Sunday Post,* 22 September 1918, 7.
52. *Bridgeport Evening Post,* 28 September 1918, 12.
53. *Bridgeport Post,* 28 September 1918.
54. National War Labor Board, Docket 132.
55. *Springfield Reporter,* 31 October 1918.

Chapter 7

1. Memo to Benedict Crowell, 13 November 1918, RG 86 MLR entry 7, box 2; *Seattle Union Record,* Final Edition, 14 November 1918, 1; National War Labor Board, Docket 132; Woman in Industry Service, "Summary of Certain Plant Investigations," RG 86, MLR entry 7, box 2, p. 2, NACP; "Rock Island

Arsenal," memo from Helen Bryan to Mary Van Kleeck, 1 July 1919, MVK, box 106, folder 1616.

2. "Jones & Lamson News," *Springfield Reporter,* 21 November 1918, 7.
3. In this entire chapter, I am indebted to Maurine Greenwald's *Women, War, and Work: The Impact of World War I on Women Workers in the United States.*
4. See, for example, William J. Cunningham, *American Railroads: Government Control and Reconstruction Policies* (Chicago: A. W. Shaw, 1922), 30, 108.
5. Greenwald, *Women, War, and Work,* 93. Figures for number of women employed come from the *Annual Report of Walker D. Hines, Director General of Railroads, 1919* (Washington, D.C., 1920), 61, and *Annual Report of W. G. McAdoo, Director General of Railroads, 1918* (Washington, D.C., 1919), 16.
6. Pauline Goldmark was the sister of the better-known Josephine Goldmark, who worked closely with Louis Brandeis in preparing legal briefs in support of protective legislation.
7. *Annual Report of W. G. McAdoo,* 16; Walker D. Hines, *The War History of American Railroads* (New Haven: Yale University Press, 1928), 168.
8. Cunningham, *American Railroads,* 111; Cunningham, a professor at the Harvard School of Business Administration, served on the staff of the director general of railroads during the period of federal control (ibid., 7).
9. *Annual Report of W. G. McAdoo,* 19.
10. Résumé of Florence Clark, RG 14, WSS, file 251, NACP.
11. Material on all of the Baltimore yards of the B&O Railroad is most readily available in BWEGM, reel 11. It may also be found in the records of the U.S. Railroad Administration, WSS, RG 14, NACP.
12. *Annual Report of Walker D. Hines,* 59.
13. *Annual Report of W. G. MacAdoo,* 21.
14. Helen Ross, Report on Inspection of Freight House, Santa Fe Railroad, Topeka, Kansas, 28 October 1918, RG 14, WSS, file 55, NACP.
15. Ibid.
16. Florence Clark, reports, memoranda, and correspondence on the Mount Clare Shops of the B&O Railroad, RG 14, WSS, file 66b, NACP.
17. RG 14, WSS, file 147, NACP.
18. Russell, "For Whom the War Is Not Over," 268.
19. Florence Clark, reports, memoranda, and correspondence on Harrisburg Division of the Pennsylvania Railroad, RG 14, WSS, files 241 and 193c, NACP.
20. Anna Crosson to Florence Clark, 21 April 1919, RG 14, entry 97, file 193c, NACP.
21. Greenwald, *Women, War, and Work,* 132–33; WSS, files 187e, 193, and 193c, NACP.
22. Cora Knisely to Florence Clark, 11 May 1919, RG 14, entry 97, WSS, file 193c, NACP.

23. Anna R. Crosson to Florence Clark, 20 May 1919, RG 14, entry 97, WSS, file 193c, NACP.
24. Complaint no. 48, RG 14, WSS, NACP.
25. Carrie B. Fearing to Director General Hines, 28 January 1919, RG 14, entry 97, box 18, file 193a, NACP.
26. Correspondence and transcript of proceedings, Records of the National War Labor Board, RG 2, Case Files, Docket 491, files 1 and 2, NACP.
27. Transcript of proceedings before the National War Labor Board, 13 March 1919, RG 2, Case Files, Docket 491, file 1, NACP.
28. Telegram, Jett Lauck to W. M. Rea, 3 December 1918, RG 2, Case Files, Docket 491, file 1, NACP.
29. Mary Van Kleeck and Mary Anderson to Jett Lauck, 10 December 1918, RG 2, Case Files, Docket 491, file 1, NACP.
30. Committee on Social and Industrial Reconstruction of the National Women's Trade Union League of America to the National War Labor Board, 11 December 1918, RG 2, Case Files, Docket 491, file 1, NACP.
31. The entire description of the hearing comes from transcript of the proceedings before the War Labor Board, "Employes vs. Cleveland Street Railway," November 1918, RG 2, Case Files, Docket 491, file 2, NACP.
32. Ibid.
33. Kennedy, *Over Here,* 138–49.
34. Dye, *As Equals,* 164.
35. *Defender,* 2 August 1919, quoted in Robb, ed., *The Negro in Chicago, 1779 to 1929,* 297.
36. Halpern, *Down on the Killing Floor,* 67; James R. Barrett, *Work and Community in the Jungle,* 219.
37. Emma Steghagan to Mary Anderson, 5 September 1919, RG 86, MLR entry 8, box 75, NACP.
38. Lehrer, *Origins of Protective Labor Legislation,* 162.
39. For an interesting discussion of this split among the feminists, see Landon R. Y. Storrs, *Civilizing Capitalism: The National Consumers' League, Women's Activism, and Labor Standards in the New Deal Era* (Chapel Hill: University of North Carolina Press, 2000), chapter 2.
40. See Mary Anderson, *Woman at Work,* chapter 19; Rose Schneiderman, "Why Labor Laws for Women?" quoted in Dye, *As Equals,* 152; and Schneiderman, *All for One,* 125–26.
41. Mary Anderson, *Woman at Work,* chapter 19.
42. See Goldin, *Understanding,* x, 197–98.
43. Ibid., 11, 17 (table 2.1).
44. See ibid., 106, 143–47.

45. Again, see the comprehensive analysis of the gender gap, ibid., especially pp. 110–17.
46. Mary Anderson, *Woman at Work,* 246–47.

Epilogue

1. Mildred Owen oral history interview transcript, *Rosie the Riveter Revisited: Women and the World War II Work Experience,* vol. 32, project director Sherna Berger Gluck (California State University, Long Beach Foundation, 1983).
2. Yung, *Unbound Feet,* 260.
3. For a detailed account of the age distribution of these women, see Goldin, *Understanding,* 153, table 5.5.
4. Using data from a 1939 Women's Bureau survey, Claudia Goldin discusses the persistence in the workforce of married and unmarried women born between 1894 and 1904. Of those who were working in 1939, the majority had worked for 75 percent of the years since beginning work (Goldin, *Understanding,* 32–34).
5. Sherna Gluck has argued convincingly that women's self-images changed as a result of war work during World War II. See her *Rosie the Riveter Revisited: Women, War and Social Change* (Boston: Twayne, 1987), chapter 12.
6. See ibid., 265–67.

A Note on the Illustrations

1. Mary Van Kleeck, "First Annual Report of the Director of the Woman in Industry Service," in *Reports of the Department of Labor,* 1919 (Washington, D.C.: GPO, 1920), 1155.
2. Walton Rawls, *Wake Up, America!: World War I and the American Poster* (New York: Abbeville Press, 1988), 149–69.

BIBLIOGRAPHY

Manuscript, Oral History, and Microfilm Collections

Amy Hewes Collection, Mount Holyoke College Archives.

Black Workers in the Era of the Great Migration, 1916–1929, James Grossman, editor; microfilm collection. [BWEGM]

Mary van Kleeck Papers, Sophia Smith Collection, Smith College. [MVK]

National Women's Trade Union League Microfilm Collection [PWTUL] (see Edward J. James, *Papers of the Women's Trade Union League and Its Principal Leaders, Guide to the Microfilm Edition,* Woodbridge, Conn.: Research Publications, Inc., 1981).

Phyllis Wheatley Association Records, Special Collections, University of Illinois at Chicago.

Records of the Chicago Urban League, University of Illinois at Chicago.

Records of the National War Labor Board, RG 2, National Archives at College Park.

Records of the Women's Bureau, RG 86, National Archives at College Park.

Records of the Women's Service Section, United States Railroad Administration, RG 14, National Archives at College Park.

Rosie the Riveter Revisited: Women and the World War II Work Experience, project director Sherna Berger Gluck, California State University, Long Beach, 1983; transcripts of interviews at Schlesinger Library, Radcliffe Institute, Harvard University.

Sophonisba Breckinridge Papers, Library of Congress.

Newspapers

Broad Ax

Bridgeport Post (also *Bridgeport Evening Post* and *Bridgeport Sunday Post)*

Defender

New York Times

Washington Post

Books and Articles

Abbott, Edith. *Women in Industry: A Study in American Economic History.* New York: D. Appleton, 1910.

Abbott, Edith, and Sophonisba Breckinridge. "Women in Industry: The Chicago Stockyards." *Journal of Political Economy* (1911): 632–54.

Adams, Frankie. "The Negro Woman in Industry." In *The Negro in Chicago,* edited by Frederic H. H. Robb, in *The Wonder Book* series. Chicago: Washington Intercollegiate Club of Chicago, 1929.

Adams, Graham. *The Age of Industrial Violence, 1910–1915: The Activities and Findings of the U.S. Commission on Industrial Relations.* New York: Columbia University Press, 1966.

Addams, Jane. *The Spirit of Youth and the City Streets.* New York: Macmillan, 1909.

Alchon, Guy. "Mary Van Kleeck and Social-Economic Planning." *Journal of Policy History* 3 (1991): 1–23.

Anderson, Karen: *Wartime Women: Sex Roles, Family Relations, and the Status of Women during World War II.* Contributions in Women's Studies, no. 20. Westport, Conn.: Greenwood Press, 1981.

Anderson, Mary. "Organizing the Bureau of Engraving and Printing Girls." *Life and Labor* 8 (1918): 11–12.

———. *Woman at Work: Autobiography of Mary Anderson as Told to Mary N. Winslow.* Minneapolis: University of Minnesota Press, 1951.

———. "Woman's Future Position in Industry." *American Industries,* December 1929, 27–29, copy in Mary Anderson papers, Schlesinger Library, Radcliffe Institute, PWTUL, reel 4.

Baillie, G. H. "Dilution of Skilled Labor, and Women in Industries." *American Machinist* 47 (1917): 951–53.

Baker, Elizabeth Faulkner. *Technology and Woman's Work.* New York: Columbia University Press, 1964.

Baker, Liva. *Felix Frankfurter.* New York: Coward-McCann, 1969.

Barrett, James R. *Work and Community in the Jungle: Chicago's Packinghouse Workers, 1894–1922.* Chicago: University of Chicago Press, 1987.

Blair, Emily Newell. *The Woman's Committee, United States Council of National Defense: An Interpretative Report, April 21, 1917 to February 27, 1919.* Washington, D.C.: Government Printing Office, 1920.

Boris, Eileen. "Tenement Homework on Army Uniforms: The Gendering of Industrial Democracy during World War I." *Labor History* 32 (1991): 231–52.

Boryczka, Raymond, and Lorin Lee Cary. *No Strength without Union: An Illustrated History of Ohio Workers, 1803–1980.* Columbus: Ohio Historical Society, 1982.

Breen, William J. "Black Women and the Great War: Mobilization and Reform in the South." In *Black Women in American History: The Twentieth Century,* edited by Darlene Clark Hine. Brooklyn: Carlson Publishing, 1990.

———. *Labor Market Politics and the Great War: The Department of Labor, the States, and the First U.S. Employment Service, 1907–1933.* Kent, Ohio: Kent State University Press, 1997.

Broehl, Wayne G., Jr. *Precision Valley: The Machine Tool Companies of Springfield, Vermont.* Englewood Cliffs, N.J.: Prentice-Hall, 1959.

Bruere, Martha Bensley. "The White Goods Strikers." *Life and Labor* 3 (1919): 73–75.

Bureau of Social Hygiene. *Housing Conditions of Employed Women in the Borough of Manhattan.* New York: n.p., 1922.

Byran, Helen. "Summary Report of Work of Women's Branch, Rock Island Arsenal." Records of the Women's Bureau, RG 86, MLR entry 7, box 2, NACP.

Butler, Elizabeth Beardsley. *Women and the Trades: Pittsburgh, 1907–1908,* edited with an introduction by Maurine Weiner Greenwald. Pittsburgh: University of Pittsburgh Press, 1984.

Camp, Helen C. *Iron in Her Soul: Elizabeth Gurley Flynn and the American Left.* Pullman: Washington State University Press, 1995.

Carpenter, Charles U. "How We Trained 5,000 Women." *Industrial Management* 55 (1918): 353–57.

Chicago Commission on Race Relations. *The Negro in Chicago: A Study of Race Relations and a Race Riot.* Chicago: University of Chicago Press, 1922.

Christy, Joe. *American Aviation: An Illustrated History.* Blue Ridge Summitt, Penn.: TAB Books, 1987.

Chubb, I. William. "Women and Machine Tools." *American Machinist* 44 (1916): 1057–62.

———. "Women in Airplane Production." *American Machinist* 48 (1918): 221–25.

Churchill, W. L. "Changing from Male to Female Help." *Industrial Management* 55 (1918): 322–24.

Clarke, Ida Clyde. *American Women and the World War.* New York: D. Appleton and Company, 1918.

"Colored Women as Industrial Workers in Philadelphia: A Study Made by the Consumers' League of Eastern Pennsylvania." 1920, 10. Division of Archives and Manuscripts, Commonwealth of Pennsylvania.

Colvin, Fred H. "Women in the Machine Shops." *American Machinist* 47 (1917): 507–12, and 48 (1918): 761–62.

Committee on Women in Industry of the Advisory Commission of the Council of National Defense. "Substitution of Women in Aircraft Production." Women in War Industries Series, no. 5, October 1918, RG 86, NACP.

Conner, Valerie J. "'The Mothers of the Race' in World War I: The National War Labor Board and Women in Industry." *Labor History* 21 (1979–80): 31–54.

———. *The National War Labor Board: Stability, Social Justice, and the Voluntary State in World War I.* Chapel Hill: University of North Carolina Press, 1983.

Consumers' League of Eastern Pennsylvania. "Colored Women as Industrial Workers in Philadelphia, 1920." Copy in Division of Archives and Manuscripts, Commonwealth of Pennsylvania.

Coser, Rose Laub, Laura S. Anker, and Andre J. Perrin. *Women of Courage: Jewish and Italian Immigrant Women in New York.* Contributions in Women's Studies, no. 173. Westport, Conn.: Greenwood Press, 1999.

Council of National Defense, Committee on Women in Industry. "The Manufacture of Army Shirts under the Home Work System, Jeffersonville, Indiana." Women in War Industries Series, no. 1, July 1918. Sophia Smith Collection, Smith College, EM Industrial Relations 1914–19, Box 15.

Council of National Defense, Women's Committee, Department of Women in Industry. "Pennsylvania Women in War Work." Sophia Smith Collection, EM Industrial Relations 1914–19, Box 15.

Crowell, Benedict. *How America Went to War.* 6 vols. New Haven: Yale University Press, 1921.

Cunningham, William James. *American Railroads: Government Control and Reconstruction Policies.* Chicago: A. W. Shaw, 1922.

Davis, Allen F. "Welfare, Reform and World War I." *American Quarterly* 19 (1967): 516–33.

Davis, Elizabeth Lindsay. *Lifting as They Climb.* 1933; reprint, New York: G. K. Hall, 1996.

———. *The Story of the Illinois Federation of Colored Women's Clubs.* 1921; reprint, New York: G. K. Hall, 1997.

Dolson, Hildegarde. "What Women Did in the Last War." Unidentified newspaper clipping, c. 1943. Records of the Women's Bureau, RG 86, MLR entry 7, Box 2, NACP.

Douglas, Paul Howard. *Real Wages in the United States, 1890–1926.* Boston: Houghton Mifflin, 1930.

DuBois, W. E. B. "The Migration of Negroes." *Crisis* 2 (1917): 63–66.

Dunbar-Nelson, Alice. "Negro Women in War Work." In Emmett Scott, ed., *Scott's Official History of the American Negro in the World War.* 1919; reprint, New York: Arno Press, 1969.

Dye, Nancy Schrom. *As Equals and as Sisters: Feminism, Unionism, and the Women's Trade Union League of New York.* Columbia: University of Missouri Press, 1980.

Earll, David S. "Our Experience with the Employment of Women." *American Machinist* 48 (1918): 240–41.

Eaton, J. M. "Comments on Training Room, Lincoln Motor Company, Detroit." Typed report to Council of National Defense, Section on Industrial Training. MVK.

Eisenstein, Sarah. *Give Us Bread but Give Us Roses: Working Women's Consciousness in the United States, 1890 to the First World War.* London: Routledge & Kegan Paul, 1983.

"Employment of Colored Women in Chicago." *Crisis* 1 (1911): 24–25.

Feldman, Egal. "Prostitution, the Alien Woman and the Progressive Imagination, 1910–1915." *American Quarterly* 19 (1967): 192–206.

Ferrell, Robert H. *Woodrow Wilson and World War I, 1917–1921.* New York: Harper & Row, 1985.

Flexner, Eleanor, and Ellen Fitzpatrick. *Century of Struggle: The Women's Rights Movement in the United States.* 1959; reprint, Cambridge: Harvard University Press, 1996.

Flynn, Elizabeth Gurley. *The Rebel Girl: The Autobiography of My First Life (1906–1926).* 1955; reprint, New York: International Publishers, 1973.

Foner, Philip S. *The Industrial Workers of the World, 1905–1917.* Vol. 4 of *History of the Labor Movement in the United States.* New York: International Publishers, 1975.

———. *Labor and World War I, 1914–1918.* Vol. 7 of *History of the Labor Movement in the Untied States.* New York: International Publishers, 1975.

———. *On the Eve of America's Entrance into World War I, 1915–1916.* Vol. 6 of *History of the Labor Movement in the United States.* New York: International Publishers, 1975.

———. *Organized Labor and the Black Worker.* New York: Praeger Publishers, 1974.

———. *Women and the American Labor Movement, From Colonial Times to the Eve of World War I.* New York: The Free Press, 1979.

———. *Women and the American Labor Movement, From World War I to the Present.* New York: The Free Press, 1980.

Foner, Philip S., and Ronald L. Lewis, editors. *The Black Worker from 1900 to 1919. Vol. 5 of The Black Worker: A Documentary History from Colonial Times to the Present.* Philadelphia: Temple University Press, 1980.

Foster, William Z. "How Life Has Been Brought into the Stockyards." *Life and Labor* 7 (1918): 63–72.

Four Years in the Underbrush: Adventures of a Working Girl in New York. New York: Charles Scribner's Sons, 1921.

Gluck, Sherna Berger. *Rosie the Riveter Revisited: Women, War, and Social Change.* Boston: Twayne, 1987.

Goldin, Claudia Dale. *Understanding the Gender Gap: An Economic History of Women.* New York: Oxford University Press, 1990.

Goldmark, Josephine. "Working Women and the Laws: A Record of Neglect." National Consumers' League publication, reprinted from *The Annals of the American Academy of Political and Social Science* 28 (1906): 261–76. MVK, box 71, folder 111.

Goldmark, Pauline. "The Facts as to Women in War Industries." *New Republic,* 29 December 1917, 251–52.

Gompers, Samuel. "Women Workers in War Time." *American Federationist* 24 (1917): 812–14.

Greenwald, Maurine. *Women, War, and Work: The Impact of World War I on Women Workers in the United States.* Westport, Conn.: Greenwood Press, 1980.

———. "Women Workers and World War I: The American Railroad Industry, A Casy Study." *Journal of Social History* 9 (1975): 154–77.

———. "Working Class Feminism and the Family Wage Ideal: The Seattle Debate on Married Women's Right to Work, 1914–1920." *Journal of American History* 76 (1989): 118–49.

Grimaldi, Lennie. *Only in Bridgeport: An Illustrated History of the Park City.* 1986; reprint, Bridgeport, Conn.: Harbor Publishing, 1993.

Grossman, James R. *Land of Hope: Chicago, Black Southerners, and the Great Migration.* Chicago: University of Chicago Press, 1989.

Grossman, Jonathan. *The Department of Labor.* New York: Praeger Publishers, 1973.

Gutman, Herbert G., and Donald H. Bell. *The New England Working Class and the New Labor History.* Urbana: University of Illinois Press, 1987.

Halpern, Rick. *Down on the Killing Floor.* Chicago: University of Illinois Press, 1997.

Harries, Meirion, and Susie Harries. *The Last Days of Innocence: America at War, 1917–1918.* New York: Random House, 1997.

Harriman, Florence J. *From Pinafores to Politics.* New York: Holt, 1923.

Harris, Glenn B. "Training Women for War Work." *American Machinist* 48 (1918): 47–48.

Harris, William H. *The Harder We Run: Black Workers Since the Civil War.* New York: Oxford University Press, 1982.

Hartness, James. *The Human Factor in Works Management.* New York: McGraw-Hill, 1912.

———. *Industrial Progress and Human Economics.* Montpelier, Vt., 1921.

Hasanovitz, Elizabeth. *One of Them: Chapters from a Passionate Autobiography.* Boston: Houghton Mifflin, 1918.

Haynes, George E. *The Negro at Work during the World War and Reconstruction: Statistics, Problems, and Policies Relating to the Greater Inclusion of Negro Wage Earners in American Industry and Agriculture.* Washington, D.C.: Government Printing Office, 1921.

Henri, Florette. *Black Migration: Movement North, 1900–1920.* Garden City, N.Y.: Anchor, 1975.

Herbst, Alma. *The Negro in the Slaughtering and Meat-Packing Industry of Chicago.* Boston: Houghton Mifflin, 1932.

Hewes, Amy. "Bridgeport on the Rebound." *The Survey* (14 October 1918): 49–51. Copy in Amy Hewes Collection.

———. *Women as Munition Makers: A Study of Conditions in Bridgeport, Connecticut.* Includes Henriette R. Walter. "Munition Workers in England and France: A Summary of Reports Issued by the British Ministry of Munitions." New York: Russell Sage Foundation, 1917.

———. "Women as Munition Makers." *The Survey* 37, no. 14 (6 January 1917): 379–85. Copy in Amy Hewes Collection.

Hines, Walker D. *Annual Report of Walker D. Hines, Director General of Railroads, 1919.* Washington, D.C.: Government Printing Office, 1920.

———. *The War History of American Railroads.* New Haven: Yale University Press, 1928.

Honey, Maureen. *Creating Rosie the Riveter: Class, Gender, and Propaganda during World War II.* Amherst: University of Massachusetts Press, 1984.

Hughes, Langston. *The Big Sea: An Autobiography.* New York: Alfred A. Knopf, 1940.

Hunter, J. V. "Service for Women in the Gisholt Shops." *American Machinist* 50 (1919): 6–10.

James, Edward J., ed. *Papers of the Women's Trade Union League and Its Principal Leaders.* Woodbridge, Conn.: Research Publications, Inc., 1981.

Jones, Adrienne Lash. "Struggle among Saints: African American Women and the YWCA, 1870–1920." In *Men and Women Adrift: The YMCA and the YWCA in the City,* edited by Nina Mjagkij and Margaret Spratt. New York: New York University Press, 1997.

Jones, Jacqueline. *Labor of Love, Labor of Sorrow: Black Women, Work, and the Family from Slavery to the Present.* 1985; reprint, New York: Vintage Books, 1986.

Karson, Marc. *American Labor Unions and Politics, 1900–1918.* Carbondale: Southern Illinois University Press, 1958.

Kelley, Florence. *Wage-Earning Women in War Time: The Textile Industry.* New York: National Consumers' League, c. 1920.

Kenneally, James J. *Women and the American Trade Unions.* St. Albans, Vt.: Eden Press, 1978.

Kennedy, David M. *Over Here: The First World War and American Society.* New York: Oxford University Press, 1980.

Knupfer, Anne Meis. "If You Can't Push, Pull, If You Can't Pull, Please Get Out of the Way: The Phyllis Wheatley Club and Home in Chicago, 1896 to 1920." *Journal of Negro History* 82 (1997): 221–31.

———. *Toward a Tenderer Humanity and a Nobler Womanhood: African American Women's Clubs in Turn-of-the-Century Chicago.* New York: New York University Press, 1996.

LaDame, Mary. "Report on the Inspection of Army and Navy Uniforms." Mayor's Commission of Women on National Defense, 31 August 1917. MVK, box 96, folder 1498.

Lehrer, Susan. *Origins of Protective Labor Legislation for Women, 1905–1925.* Albany: SUNY Press, 1987.

Livesey, Anthony. *The Historical Atlas of World War I.* New York: Henry Holt, 1994.

Malkiel, Theresa Serber. *The Diary of a Shirtwaist Striker.* Ithaca: ILR Press, 1990.

Manley, Basil M., and Francis Patrick Walsh. *Final Report of the Commission on Industrial Relations.* Chicago: Barnard and Miller, 1915.

McAdoo, W. G. *Annual Report of W. G. McAdoo, Director General of Railroads, 1918.* Washington, D.C.: Government Printing Office, 1919.

McDowell, Mary E. "Mothers and Night Work." *The Survey* 39 (1917): 335–36.

McMurry, Linda O. *To Keep the Waters Troubled: The Life of Ida B. Wells.* New York: Oxford University Press, 1998.

Meyerowitz, Joanne J. *Women Adrift: Independent Wage Earners in Chicago, 1880–1930.* Chicago: University of Chicago Press, 1988.

Morrison, C. J. "Safeguarding Women in Machine Shops." *American Machinist* 47 (1917): 843.

National Industrial Conference Board. "Wartime Employment of Women in the Metal Trades." Research Report no. 8. Boston: NICB, 1918.

National Urban League. *40th Anniversary Year Book, 1950.* New York, 1951.

National War Labor Board. "Employees vs. The Cleveland Street Railway Company." Records of the National War Labor Board, RG 2, Case Files, Docket 491, NACP.

———. *National War Labor Board Docket: A Compilation of the Actions of the National War Labor Board, 1918–1919.* Docket 132, vol. 1. Washington, D.C.: 1919. Records of the War Labor Board, RG 2, NACP.

National Women's Trade Union League. "The Eight Hour Day for Women." Chicago: NWTUL, 1915.

The Negro in Chicago, edited by Frederic H. H. Robb in *The Wonder Book* series. Chicago: Washington Intercollegiate Club of Chicago, 1929.

Nestor, Agnes. *Woman's Labor Leader.* Rockford, Ill.: Bellevue Books, 1954.

New York State Committee on Women in Industry, Council of National Defense. "Home-Work on Naval Garments, Brooklyn Navy Yard, N.Y." Typed report, 22 November 1917. Sophonisba Breckinridge Papers, Library of Congress.

Norton, Esther. "Women in War Industries." *New Republic,* 15 December 1917, 179–81.

Oberdeck, Kathryn J. "'Not Pink Teas': The Seattle Working Class Women's Movement, 1905–1918." *Labor History* 32 (1991): 193–230.

Odencrantz, Louise C. *Italian Women in Industry: A Study of Conditions in New York City.* New York: Russell Sage Foundation, 1919.

Odencrantz, Louise Christine, and Zenas L. Potter. *Industrial Conditions in Springfield, Illinois; A Survey by the Committee on Women's Work and the Department of Surveys and Exhibits, Russell Sage Foundation.* New York: Department of Surveys and Exhibits, Russell Sage Foundation, 1916.

O'Neill, William L. *Everyone Was Brave: The Rise and Fall of Feminism in America.* Chicago: Quadrangle, 1969.

Orleck, Annelise. *Common Sense and a Little Fire: Women and Working-Class Politics in the United States, 1900–1965.* Chapel Hill: University of North Carolina Press, 1995.

O'Shea, Peter F. "A Shop Training School for Girls." *Industrial Management* 58 (1919): 213–15.

Parrish, Michael E. *Felix Frankfurter and His Times: The Reform Years.* New York: Free Press, 1982.

Payne, Elizabeth Anne. *Reform, Labor, and Feminism: Margaret Dreier Robins and the Women's Trade Union League.* Chicago: University of Illinois Press, 1988.

Peake, May. "The Woman Machinist: Her Accomplishments and Her Possibilities." *Life and Labor* 9 (1919): 326–29.

Pearlman, Lester M. "Ordnance Workers in 1918 and 1943." *Monthly Labor Review* 57 (1943): 1074–81.

Rawls, Walton. *Wake Up, America! World War I and the American Poster.* New York: Abbeville Press, 1988.

Reed, Christopher Robert. *The Chicago NAACP and the Rise of Black Professional Leadership, 1910–1966.* Bloomington: Indiana University Press, 1997.

Rowe, Lily Lykes. "Mary Anderson: How an Immigrant Girl Rose to High Federal Office." *Ladies Home Journal,* August 1920, 61–62. Copy in the Mary Anderson Papers, reel 4.

Ruiz, Vicki L. *From Out of the Shadows: Mexican Women in Twentieth-Century America.* New York: Oxford University Press, 1998.

Russell, Ruth M. "For Whom the War Is Not Over." *Life and Labor* 8 (1918): 266–68.

Salem, Dorothy. *To Better Our World: Black Women in Organized Reform, 1890–1920.* In *Black Women in United States History,* general editor Darlene Clark Hine. Brooklyn: Carlson Publishing, 1990.

Schneider, Dorothy, and Carl J. Schneider. *Into the Breach: American Women Overseas in World War I.* New York: Viking, 1991.

Schneiderman, Rose. *All for One.* New York: P. S. Eriksson, 1967.

———. "A Cap Maker's Story." *The Independent* 58 (1905): 935–38.

———. "The White Goods Workers of New York: Their Struggle for Human Conditions." *Life and Labor* 3 (1913): 132–36.

Scott, Emmett J. "Additional Letters of Negro Migrants of 1916–1918." *Journal of Negro History* 4 (1919): 412–65.

———. "Letters of Negro Migrants of 1916–1918." *Journal of Negro History* 4 (1919): 290–340.

———. *Negro Migration during the War.* Preliminary Economic Studies of the War no. 16, edited by David Kinley. New York: Oxford University Press, 1920.

———, ed. *Scott's Official History of the American Negro in the World War.* 1919; reprint, New York: Arno Press, 1969.

Shrader, Charles Reginald, ed. *Reference Guide to United States Military History, 1865–1919.* New York: Facts on File, 1993.

Smith, Ethel M. "At Last—A National Woman's Labor Bureau." *Life and Labor* 8 (1918): 159–61.

Spear, Allan H. *Black Chicago: The Making of a Negro Ghetto, 1890–1920.* Chicago: University of Chicago Press, 1967.

Stein, Leon, editor. *Out of the Sweatshop: The Struggle for Industrial Democracy.* New York: Quadrangle, 1977.

Sterling, Dorothy. *Black Foremothers: Three Lives.* New York: Feminist Press, 1988.

Storrs, Landon R. Y. *Civilizing Capitalism: The National Consumers' League, Women's Activism, and Labor Standards in the New Deal Era.* Chapel Hill: University of North Carolina Press, 2000.

Strickland, Arvarh E. *History of the Chicago Urban League.* Urbana: University of Illinois Press, 1966.

Sullivan, Olive M. "The Women's Part in the Stockyards Organization Work." *Life and Labor* 7 (1918): 102, 104.

Tentler, Leslie Woodcock. *Wage-Earning Women: Industrial Work and Family Life in the United States, 1900–1930.* New York: Oxford University Press, 1979.

Terrell, Mary Church. *A Colored Woman in a White World.* 1940; reprint, New York: Arno Press, 1980.

Thomas, Richard W. *Life for Us Is What We Make It: Building Black Community in Detroit, 1915–1945.* Bloomington: Indiana University Press, 1992.

Trattner, Walter I. *Crusade for the Children: A History of the National Child Labor Committee and Child Labor Reform in America.* Chicago: Quadrangle, 1970.

Trotter, Joe William, and Earl Lewis, eds. *African Americans in the Industrial Age: A Documentary History, 1915–1945.* Boston: Northeastern University Press, 1996.

Turner, Mrs. V. B. "Women in the Mechanical Trades." *Monthly Labor Review* 7 (1918): 682–91.

"Uniforms to be Taken Out of Sweatshops." *Life and Labor* 6 (1917): 158.

U.S. Department of Labor, Women's Bureau. "Employment of Women in Hazardous Industries." Bulletin no. 6, Washington, D.C., 1921.

———. "Health Problems of Women in Industry." Bulletin no. 18, Washington, D.C., 1921.

———. "Home Work in Bridgeport, Connecticut." Bulletin no. 9, Washington, D.C., 1919.

———. "Negro Women in Industry." Bulletin no. 20, Washington, D.C., 1922.

———. "Negro Women in Industry in 15 States." Bulletin no. 70, Washington, D.C., 1929.

———. "The New Position of Women in Industry." Bulletin no. 12, Washington, D.C., 1920.

———. "Proposed Employment of Women during the War in the Industries of Niagara Falls, New York." Bulletin no. 1, Washington, D.C., 1918.

———. "Some Effects of Legislation Limiting Hours of Work for Women." Bulletin no. 15, Washington, D.C., 1921.

———. "Standards for the Employment of Women in Industry." Bulletin no. 3, Washington, D.C., 1921.

———. "Wages of Candy Makers in Philadelphia in 1919." Bulletin no. 4, Washington, D.C., 1919.

U.S. Department of Labor, Women in Industry Series, Bureau of Labor Statistics.

"Summary Report on the Conditions of Women and Child Wage Earners." Series no. 5, Bulletin no. 175, Washington, D.C., 1915.

U.S. Department of Labor, Women's Bureau. "Women Street Car Conductors and Ticket Agents." Bulletin no. 11. Washington, D.C., 1921.

U.S. War Department Committee on Education and Training. Final Report. Washington, D.C., 1919.

Van Kleeck, Mary. *Artificial Flower Makers.* New York: Survey Association, 1913.

———. "First Annual Report of the Director of the Woman in Industry Service." In *Reports of the Department of Labor, 1919.* Washington, D.C.: Government Printing Office, 1920.

———. "The National Importance of Woman's Work." In Newsletter of the Woman's Committee, Council of National Defense, 15 September 1918. Copy in Records of the Women's Bureau, RG 86, MLR entry 1, box 1, NACP.

———. "New Standards for Negro Women in Industry." *Life and Labor* 9 (1919): 134–35.

———. "Proposed Employment of Women during the War in the Industries of Niagara Falls, New York." *Monthly Labor Review* (January 1919): 231–46; also published as U.S. Department of Labor, Woman in Industry Service, Bulletin no. 1, November 1918.

———. "Report on the Employment of Women in the Storage and Warehousing Depots of the United States Army." War Industries Board Storage Bulletin no. 9. Typed report in MVK, box 72, folder 1125.

———. "Trade Union Women." *New Republic,* 16 November 1918, 74.

———. *Women in the Bookbinding Trade.* New York: Survey Association, 1913.

———. "Women in the Munition Industries." *Life and Labor* 8 (1918): 113–22.

Van Kleeck, Mary, et al. *A Seasonal Industry: A Study of the Millinery Trade in New York.* New York: Russell Sage Foundation, 1917.

Viall, W. A. "Employment of Women in Our Industries." *American Machinist* 48 (1918): 909–11.

Washington. Forrester B. "Reconstruction and the Colored Woman." *Life and Labor* 9 (1919): 3–7.

"The War and Votes for Women." *New Republic,* 10 August 1918, 33–35.

Weber, Gustavus Adolphus. *The Women's Bureau: Its History, Activities, and Organization.* 1923; reprint, New York: AMS Press, 1974.

Webster, George W. "A Physiological Basis for the Shorter Working Day for Women." U.S. Department of Labor, Women's Bureau, Bulletin no. 14, Washington, D.C., February 1921.

West, Rebecca. "Mothering the Munition Maker." *New Republic,* 6 October 1917, 266–69.

Wilson, William B., et al. *The Anvil and the Plow: A History of the United States Department of Labor.* Washington, D.C.: Government Printing Office, 1963.

Wolfson, Theresa. "Trade Union Activities of Women." *Annals of the American Academy of Political and Social Science* 143 (1929): 120–31.

"Woman in Industry." *New Republic,* 26 October 1918, 365–66.

Woman in Industry Service. "Summary of Certain Plant Investigations." Records of the Women's Bureau, RG 86, MLR entry 7, box 2, NACP.

"The Woman in Industry Service." Typed history, Records of the Women's Bureau; RG 86, MLR entry 1, box 2, NACP.

"The Woman Street Car Conductor—Shall She Have Fair Play?" *Life and Labor* 9 (1919): 14–16.

"Women Street Car Conductors to Be Reinstated." *Life and Labor* 9 (1919): 98–100.

Woods, Robert A., and Albert J. Kennedy. *Young Working Girls: A Summary of Evidence from Two Thousand Social Workers.* Boston: Houghton Mifflin, 1913.

Yung, Judy. *Unbound Feet: A Social History of Chinese Women in San Francisco.* Berkeley: University of California Press, 1995.

———. *Unbound Voices: A Documentary History of Chinese Women in San Francisco.* Berkeley: University of California Press, 1999.

INDEX

References to illustrations appear in boldface type.